GRIAND...
PHOTO...
PHOTO...

DÁ MHNAOI CHEILE.
WIFE. - FEMME.

Sighniu an tSealbhóra...
...IRE OF BEARER...

Agus Sighniu a Mhná Céile.
And of his Wife.
Et de sa Femme.

IRISH ... ...STATE

Life with Mae

Great Lakes Books

*A complete listing of the books in this series
can be found online at wsupress.wayne.edu*

Life with Mae

A Detroit Family Memoir

NEAL SHINE

Wayne State University Press Detroit

© 2007 by Wayne State University Press, Detroit, Michigan 48201.
All rights reserved. No part of this book may be reproduced without formal
permission. Manufactured in the United States of America.
12 11 10 09 08   6 5 4 3 2

Library of Congress Cataloging-in-Publication Data
Shine, Neal.
Life with Mae : a Detroit family memoir / Neal Shine.
p. cm. — (Great Lakes books)
ISBN-13: 978-0-8143-3298-6 (cloth : alk. paper)
ISBN-10: 0-8143-3298-6 (cloth : alk. paper)
ISBN-13: 978-0-8143-3299-3 (paper : alk. paper)
ISBN-10: 0-8143-3299-4 (paper : alk. paper)
1. Shine, Neal—Childhood and youth. 2. Shine, Neal—Family. 3. Irish
American families—Michigan—Detroit—Biography. 4. Irish American
Catholics—Michigan—Detroit—Biography. 5. Shine, Mae, 1909–1987.
6. Mothers—Michigan—Detroit—Biography. 7. Women immigrants—
Michigan—Detroit—Biography. 8. Detroit (Mich.)—Biography. 9. Detroit
(Mich.)—Social life and customs—20th century. 10. Carrick-on-Shannon
(Ireland)—Biography. I. Title.
F574.D49I67 2007
974'.3400491620092—dc22
[B]
2007027359

All photos courtesy of the Shine family's personal collection.

Poems by Michael J. MacManus have been reprinted by permission of the
poet's estate.

∞ The paper used in this publication meets the minimum requirements
of the American National Standard for Information Sciences—
Permanence of Paper for Printed Library Materials, ANSI Z39.48-1984.

Designed and typeset by Maya Rhodes
Composed in Coronet and Sabon

For Phyllis,
a chroidhe dhil, beloved heart,
for a lifetime of love without measure.

Contents

Acknowledgments

I am grateful to my brothers, Jim and Bill, and their wives, Barbara and Pat, for their help in this effort. Bill and Jim obligingly dragged through Ireland and England with me and I treasure that time together and the chance to revisit our mother's childhood as well as our own.

I thank Jim for being wise enough to have Seamus Conlon, my mother's youngest brother, talk at length on tape about life in Carrick-on-Shannon. Those recollections were invaluable in providing context for large parts of the story.

My mother's sisters—Kitty, Midge, and Gertie—and their husbands, George Paris, Reg Gurney, and Pat Gawley, opened their homes and their hearts to us during our visit to England. This story is richer for their love and their memories, which they generously shared.

None of this, of course, would have been possible if Jane Hoehner and Kathy Wildfong of Wayne State University Press had not said yes very early in the process. I am deeply grateful to them both. My thanks also to managing editor Kristin Harpster Lawrence and copyeditor Polly Kummel for their valuable advice and suggestions, and to production editor Carrie Downes Teefey for shepherding the book to its completion.

I am indebted to my wife, Phyllis, for gently prodding me to get the manuscript finished and then carefully reading it in its various stages, sending me back to recheck facts, uncomplicate compound sentences, and lighten up tedious passages.

My daughter, Peg, my daughter-in-law, Kim North Shine, and my son Dan were always ready to drop whatever they were doing whenever I asked them for help in checking elusive facts or running down obscure bits of information. I thank them for that.

I am profoundly indebted to my friend and former colleague Berl Falbaum for his enthusiasm for the book from its earliest stages, for his encouragement and for his suggestions and his judicious editing.

My dear friend Jane Briggs-Bunting, director of the School of Journalism at Michigan State University as well as my former student and later my colleague at the *Free Press* and at Oakland University, played a special part in this effort. I am deeply grateful.

Javan Kienzle, the "Closet Colleen," *Free Press* colleague and dear friend, was a constant during the entire process. Encouraging at the beginning, supportive in the middle, and always confident. I thank her for sharing her talent as an editor and for her continued friendship.

Maury Kelman and Bernie Klein were generous with their advice and suggestions about the manuscript, and I value their help and their friendship.

Detroit Free Press librarian Chris Kucharski was always available and accommodating whenever I needed her to check a fact or find something for me in the paper's archives.

Patsy Mann, Mae Shine's dear friend and neighbor, who brought her own measure of Irish devilment to the relationship, was helpful in tracking down sources for me and in contributing her own memories of Mae.

Thanks to Ned McGrath, of the Archdiocese of Detroit, for helping me with the Legion of Decency movie listings.

There were nights when my neighbors in Stoney Point, Ontario, Jeanne and Jim Boyes, decided that sometimes eating is more important than writing. I thank them for the home-cooked meals.

The material about Carrick poet Susan Mitchell was taken from her biography, *Red-Headed Rebel* by Hilary Pyle (Woodfield Press). Mark Bence-Jones's *Twilight of the Ascendancy* (Constable & Company Ltd.) was a valuable source for information about the manor houses of the Anglo-Irish in the country's history. *Leitrim and the Croppies 1776–1804* by Gerard MacAtasney (Carrick-on-Shannon and District Historical Society) provided an important insight into life in Leitrim in the eighteenth and nineteenth centuries.

For the details about Moyvane/Newtownsandes and its various name changes I thank T. J. Barrington and his book, *Discovering Kerry.*

Carrick-on-Shannon—Remembered, published in 1998 by the Carrick-on-Shannon and District Historical Society, was a vital resource for information about Carrick, its history, and its people. For this I thank the staff and editors of the book, especially Evelyn McCabe, John Rooney, Billy Gilligan, Sean Gill, Patricia Molloy, and the late Des Cox. Members of the Historical Society, Evelyn McCabe, Mike Joe Mahon, Dermot MacNabb, John Bredin, Arthur Kellitt, and the late Des Smith, took time to meet with us and patiently answer our questions about Carrick-on-Shannon, past and present. Their help is deeply appreciated.

My brothers and I are grateful to Rosaleen and Joe Dolan, proprietors of the Bush Hotel, for the warm hospitality during our visit to Carrick-on-Shannon, and to Rosaleen's father, Arthur Laird, for his memories of life in Carrick.

Also in Carrick, Paddy Boyle, Gertie Conlon's godfather, and his wife, Mary, were more than gracious with their time and hospitality, as were John and Rita Costello.

Claire Moran and James Faughnan, solicitors at Cathal L. Flynn & Co., whose law offices occupy the premises in St. George's Terrace that had been the home of the Bradshaw family where my mother worked from 1923 to 1927, spent a morning showing us through the old house. We thank them for this kindness.

That the people of Carrick-on-Shannon made us feel welcome

in their shops and in their homes was not something that surprised us. Our mother made sure we understood the generosity and openness of the people of Carrick long before we saw the town for the first time.

The folks at Failte Ireland, the country's tourist agency, patiently searched out information for us in Carrick and Dublin without ever making us feel like we were pestering them.

And finally, I cannot find words adequate to express the extent of the joy that my children and my grandchildren have brought to my life: daughter Judy, her husband, Jack Heuvelman, and their children, Sara and Ken; son Jim, his wife, Dede, and their children, Colin, Caitlin, and Neal; daughter Sue, her husband, Rodger Epp, and their children, Austen, Travis, Clare, and Audrey; son Tom, his wife, Sharon, and their children, Conor, Alaina, and Laura; daughter Peggy, her husband, Larry Berkowski, and their children, Ted, Neala, and Juliana; and son Dan, his wife, Kim, and their children, Maura and Niall. Each of them is an unending source of happiness, and spending time with them in Carrick-on-Shannon in the summer of 2004 is a golden memory I will cherish forever.

Prologue

When Mae Shine died in 1987, we found the green box where she had kept it for more than fifty years—in the bottom drawer of her dresser on top of a faded chenille bedspread. The box is shaped like a half moon, twelve inches across at its widest part and a bit more than three inches deep. The patterned silk covering was once a rich emerald green but has long since faded and is stained in places with water marks. The inside of the lid is lined with pleated white silk that has yellowed over the years, and the narrow ribbons that connected the lid to the box are torn away. Not an entirely impressive repository for the odds and ends that were the tangible fragments of the life of Mary Ellen Conlon Shine.

It had been part of a vanity set—hand mirror, comb, nail file, buffer, shoehorn, and a small oval tray with a crocheted doily encased in glass. Neither my brothers nor I have any idea where the set came from. A wedding gift, perhaps, or something my father bought her. But our collective memory—I was born in 1930, Jim in 1932, and Bill in 1936—is that it was always there, on top of the dresser pushed up against the big mirror.

We lived at 635 Beniteau then, south of East Jefferson, not far from the Detroit River. It's the first house I remember. In 1938 we moved from Beniteau to 1532 Lycaste, a few blocks away. In 1948 we stopped being renters and bought our first house, 1119 Wayburn, in Grosse Pointe Park.

At some point in the early 1940s my mother must have decided the box was getting timeworn and exiled it to the bottom drawer. She left the rest of the set, some pieces of which survive, on the dresser top.

As far back as the Beniteau house, we remember the box as the place she kept "her stuff," but our memory is that it was never a secret hiding place, something off-limits to children. We would sometimes take the box off the dresser and sort through the things she kept in it, none of it of much interest to a kid. Her only admonition was to put everything back in the box when we were finished. She continued to add to the box even after we were grown and had moved away.

When she died, the box held more than two hundred items, mostly, but not limited to, old letters and snapshots, religious cards, utility receipts, and brittle newspaper clippings, many with ragged edges, evidence that they had been torn instead of scissored from the pages of the paper.

Trying to determine whether there was any reasonable explanation for why she saved one school assignment or a particular newspaper clipping or why she decided one prayer card was more special than scores of others is a mostly futile exercise. There seemed to be no minimum standard for inclusion, no theme, no clear indication that any of it reflected her sense of historical importance.

Some contents certainly made sense: letters from her mother and father in Ireland—tied together with butcher string—and a handful of other things with a direct link to what she considered an important event in the life of the Shine family. But most of it simply defied reasonable explanation. The closest we can come to motive is that if she felt like putting something in the box, she did.

In a very real way, the box and its contents typify, very directly, how she moved through life—providing little evidence that the things she did had any basis in logic. If her strategy was to keep all of us guessing about her, it worked.

I'm sure she saved the letters from her parents not so much for the sentiments they contained but because they were her last, tenuous connection to the life she had left in Ireland, a life she would never have again. In letters sprinkled with initialed entreaties—TG (thank God), DV (Deo volente, God willing)—they talked to her about her brothers and sisters, some born after she left home, and kept her up-to-date on the recently deceased in Carrick-on-Shannon—Kitty Hamilton, Johnny Moran's mother, "old" Willie Thompson, all RIP.

The box contains a note, an unpunctuated message she had written in pencil on a sheet torn from a pad of paper used for keeping score in card games. "We—They" was printed three times across the top of the sheet and separated by vertical lines. It was a promotional item provided by the Riverside Storage and Cartage Company. On the small sheet she wrote:

if I'm not home make some cheese sandwiches

It's clear she did not save the note to impress future generations with the depth of her concern that her children be provided with regular, balanced, and nutritious meals. She probably kept it because of what I had written on the other side of the sheet, something that spoke to my zeal to sell as many tickets as possible for a St. Rose school raffle to raise money for the foreign missions. I was apparently able to convince Bill, my youngest brother, to assist me in this worthwhile and blessed endeavor. On the sheet, I wrote, also in pencil, "I will sell 1 book of tickets for Neal Shine. If I don't he may hit me 50 times."

It was signed "B. Shine," more, I'm sure, because of the threat than from any desire on Bill's part to save pagan babies, which was always the ultimate goal in foreign mission fund-raisers. I like to think she saved the note because she was profoundly touched by her oldest son's efforts, however questionable the method, to bring the gift of St. Rose–style Christianity to heathen infants in another land.

A very small, but certainly not representative, sampling of the contents of the box includes a September 21, 1930, receipt from

Cottage Hospital in Grosse Pointe Farms for $46, the cost of my birth seven days earlier; a ragged clipping from a 1929 *Detroit Free Press* that contained the last poem of Robert Burns, written for the young woman who had cared for him in his final illness; an August 15, 1939, receipt from the Detroit and Cleveland Navigation Company for $3, the cost of a stateroom for the overnight run from Detroit to Cleveland; a ticket good for one fare on the old Detroit United Railway; the program for the 1948 St. Rose High School junior prom; a 1936 funeral card for Billy Ward, a neighborhood kid who died young; a religious card commemorating the first Solemn Mass in 1948 of Father Frank Burns, who had also grown up in the neighborhood; my report card from the second semester of my freshman year at the University of Detroit, five C's and a B, a 2.18 (strong C) grade point average; and my bronze-colored aluminum "War Service 1945" medal bearing the likeness of Dwight Eisenhower and attesting to my "extraordinary patriotic achievement in the Boy Scout–Gen. Eisenhower Waste Paper Campaign, March–April 1945." She might not have been as eager to include the medal in her collection if she had known how the Scouts of Troop 20 had exceeded the number of pounds of wastepaper they had been assigned to gather: we buried ourselves in the old newspapers before the truck was weighed at the salvage yard.

There is a one-paragraph news item about a streetcar motorman who took his life by cutting his throat with a razor in the front room of his house on Clark Street while his wife watched, presumably in horror, although the writer managed to resist the cliché.

The box also held a pair of my baby shoes, ankle-high white leather with black patent leather bottoms and no laces, and some remnants of my early attempts at scholarship: grade-school book reports and an eighth-grade social studies test titled "A Divided Nation: Struggling over Slavery." There were nine questions. I got seven wrong and did not answer the ninth. There was also a third-grade spelling book in which I was still printing the *N* in Neal backward, and an ungraded five-page report on the short story with *Late* written at the top by my teacher.

The box also contained some random cuttings of my early journalistic efforts as a reporter at the *Detroit Free Press*: the final installment of a three-part series that I did in 1960 on a police scandal in Chicago, and a story on the 1957 murder in Muttonville, Michigan, of a country singer, a man I cleverly described as "the Elvis Presley of the Thumb," who had been shot by a jealous husband.

Since none of it represented what I considered an honest cross-section of my efforts as a writer for the *Free Press,* I think she may have kept them against the day she could add more provocative samples of my writing to reinforce the validity of her belief that her children were always capable of better work.

Based on the old letters in the box, at some unrecorded and unexplained point in her first years in America she ceased being May and became Mae.

The collected works of my father's romantic correspondence—one letter and a postcard written in 1929 and stored in the same green box—have him addressing her as May. In September 1930 she was listed on my birth certificate as Mae, having slipped quietly between the two spellings sometime in the intervening year. It was obviously not a defining moment in her life because, as far as any of us can recall, she never mentioned it.

Whatever the reason for the change, she was, from that point forward, Mae. To her children she was simply Ma and to her friends, neighbors, and everybody else who knew her, even slightly, she was always Ma Shine.

She was grandmother to fifteen and, ultimately, great-grandmother to thirty-three, including her namesake, Mae Conlon Shine, born in 2003 to Bill's son Stephen, and his wife, Melinda. Ma was also surrogate mother and grandmother to countless others with whom she shared no blood ties.

Mae Shine was the oldest of thirteen children. She went into service as a domestic when she was fourteen. She left Carrick-on-Shannon, County Leitrim, Ireland, at eighteen because even then she understood that if she stayed in Ireland, she could look forward to a life for herself and her children little better than the one she was already living. In America, she believed—correctly, it turned out—all things were possible.

She came to Duluth, Minnesota, in 1927, sponsored by the daughter of family friends back in Ireland, a woman who was, apparently, also a madam. This bit of information was something the woman prudently neglected to mention in her correspondence with my grandparents when she agreed to sponsor their daughter's immigration to America.

Mae Conlon was able to find work in Duluth doing what she knew how to do and what she had done in Ireland: taking care of other people's houses. She worked as a housekeeper for a succession of Jewish families in Duluth and later in Detroit, making a shambles of their dietary laws and religious observances, practices she decided were contrived not so much to elevate her employers to some kind of higher spiritual plane as they were to simply create more work for her. Two sets of dishes, indeed. So she ignored most of it, dismissing it all quite casually as "make-work."

That she moved from one Jewish family to another on the basis of highly questionable letters of recommendation gives full credence to the operative principle of "better them than us."

To call Mae Shine outspoken would require a much broader definition of the term as it is generally used. She kept nothing to herself. If something was on her mind, she was never reluctant to share it. People who asked for her opinion on anything had best be prepared for a brutally honest answer. When her friend Mary Nolan asked her after Mass one Sunday if her new dress made her behind look fat, Mae told Mary, "No fatter than it always looks." Mary Nolan, satisfied with the answer, kept the dress, and the friendship endured.

Mae was also a harsh and often caustic critic. When I was writing a column for the *Free Press,* she always felt free, when her perception of truth required it, to weigh in regularly with observations like, "Pretty weak offering this morning." When I would respond by telling her my editors liked it, she'd say something about the readers being better served if the paper hired editors who knew something about writing.

But when criticism came from other sources, she became my most committed defender. A reader once called my columns "tedious exercises in phony Irish bonhomie." When I told Ma about the letter, she asked me for the writer's name and address so she could write him a note and discuss the matter with him. I refused, telling her I was old enough to fight my own battles. She said something about my record being open to question in that regard. I also think she might have considered the man's comment a slur on the Irish and was more ready to confront him on that point than to engage in any debate in defense of my writing skills.

Like my father, she was a bedrock Democrat and dismissed conservatives as people who embraced that philosophy because they always seemed to be the ones with the most to conserve. She denied being a "yellow dog" Democrat, a party loyalist who would vote for a yellow dog as long as it was on the Democratic ticket. But that, apparently, was the only place she was willing to draw the line.

She hated war, and at the height of the violent troubles in Northern Ireland, she would neither join nor contribute to any Irish organization she suspected might use her money, as she put it, "to buy bullets to kill some other mother's son." She had no patience with people who disliked others because of their race or where they came from. She never forgot that she was in this country at the sufferance of those who had been here generations before she arrived. Nor did she hesitate to remind her Irish-born friends of that—often in harsh terms—whenever they began talking what she called "race trash."

She was also confounded by the concerns of some of her friends about homosexuality. She had a number of gay friends, although she confided to me once, when I was about eighteen, that there was no such thing as homosexuality when she was a girl, prompting a rare son-to-mother discussion of the facts of life. When the discussion ended, she grudgingly conceded, "Well, maybe so, but there were never any in Ireland." I decided that mentioning Oscar Wilde would simply confuse things further.

A woman of enormous certainties, she believed that the meek would, indeed, inherit the earth but that their chances would improve measurably if they pushed their way to the front of the line when the will was being read.

In the fall of 1987 she had been living at our house—temporarily, she insisted—for what turned out to be the last two weeks of her life. When she became ill one evening, we decided she needed to go to St. John Hospital. She was having difficulty breathing, and we called the emergency medical service in Grosse Pointe Park.

The fire department lieutenant in charge of the squad, Lee Fallieres, a fellow parishioner at St. Ambrose who knew she lived on Wayburn, said, when he saw her in bed at our house on Bedford, "Ma Shine! What are you doing here?"

"I sleep around," she replied.

While Fallieres and the other officers were carefully lifting her stretcher over the second-floor railing, she looked anxiously down at the long stairway below and said: "Lee, if you drop me, I swear I'll sue the damned city for every nickel it's got."

Her doctor, Kevin Grady, admitted her and told us he would call if her condition worsened. It did. Early the next morning he said we should come to the hospital.

On the afternoon of November 8, 1987, she died at St. John Hospital, surrounded in the small room by children and grandchildren. She opened her eyes, looked at us standing near her bed, and told us it was good of us to come but really not necessary. Then she smiled at us, closed her eyes, and, after a few minutes, stopped breathing. She was seventy-eight.

Every night of her life, kneeling next to her bed, she had said a prayer for a happy death, asking God to "grant that I may pass my days in the practice of holiness and justice, and that I may deserve to quit this world in the peace of a good conscience, and in the embraces of Thy love."

That she died exactly the way she wanted was not something that surprised any of us. In her final moments she dealt with death the way she dealt with everything else in life—on her own terms. None of us expected that death would change any of that. When it came to the question of passing her days "in the practice of holiness and justice," we agreed that she met the standard and richly deserved to be able to quit the world in the peace of a good conscience.

Even Kevin Grady, who had been one of her doctors for only about a year, seemed to understand that. He was a specialist in pulmonary medicine and was in the same practice as another doctor who had been treating her. The day she saw him for the first time, he walked into the examination room wearing khaki pants, an open-collared polo shirt, brown boat shoes, and no socks. She looked at him, not quite willing to believe what she was seeing. "How the hell old are you?" she demanded, convinced he was some college kid working part time at the doctor's office to help pay his tuition at medical school. He was thirty-two but could easily have passed for someone ten years younger.

He is the son of Dan Grady, a classmate of mine from the University of Detroit, and his wife, Margaret, who have been my friends for more than fifty years. Dan Grady was my entire photographic staff when I was photo editor of the *Varsity News* at U of D. I never mentioned to my mother that her doctor's father was, in those years, a photographer of moderate skill. One of her fervently held beliefs was that what is bred in the bone will out, and I was hesitant to burden her with any more information about her new young doctor, whose sense of fashion was already suspect.

She died from complications of a lung disorder that had been diagnosed about eight years earlier. The doctors told her it was inoperable, and, after what seemed an endless succession of tests and scans, they finally determined that she could have as many as two years left and that she should concentrate on enjoying them.

In the days following the diagnosis, she planned her funeral down to the last detail. She told us she wanted her grandsons to be her pallbearers and insisted that we have a big party after the Mass and invite everyone she ever knew. As far as the church service went, she told us she wanted no ponderous funeral music, no "Dies Irae," because it was not going to be a "Day of Wrath." She ordained that there would be Irish music—jigs, reels, and slides, no laments—to see her off on this final journey. And she promised to come back and haunt any person who tried to sing "Danny Boy." Fiddler Mick Gavin and piper Al Purcell saw to it that the music was spirited, and there was an unusual amount of foot tapping in St. Ambrose Church that morning.

She asked that she be cremated and that part of her ashes be buried with my father, Patrick Shine, in Detroit's Mt. Olivet Cemetery. He died in 1969. She asked us to take the rest of her ashes and spread them in the Shannon by the old stone bridge in Carrick. "It's where I started and it's where I want to end up," she told us.

Then she concentrated on cramming all the living she could muster into the next eight years, never slowing down, never looking back to see if death was gaining on her.

Six months before she died, she made one last trip to England to visit her sisters and their families. When she came home after that visit, she told us how much it had tired her. "I think this was probably my last trip," she said. But we had heard that from her before and learned not to take any of it at face value. This time she was right.

What follows is our remembrance of Mae Conlon Shine's remarkable and often outrageous life, painted in bold strokes, to help keep her memory fresh in the minds of those who knew and loved her and to give some sense of who she was to those who do not remember her, especially her great-grandchildren. It is also for those who never met her but who had in their lives a wonderful woman like her, a mother, an aunt, a grandmother, women who were always ready to share their abundant love, their vibrant spirit, and their gift of laughter. I hope it will be a reminder of just how substantial our debt is to these remarkable women.

Mary Ellen Conlon Shine on her wedding day, June 29, 1929

Life with Mae

The Beginning

On January 27, 1909, Katie Dolan, the local midwife, was summoned to the small laborer's cottage on the Leitrim Road, in Carrick-on-Shannon, County Leitrim, Ireland, to attend at the birth of Mary Ellen Conlon, the first child of Bridget Downs Conlon and James Conlon. Twelve more children would be born to Bridget and James, two of them after Mary Ellen was having children of her own. Two, Sarah and Bridget, died within days of their birth.

Nobody in the family is quite sure how James Conlon was earning a living when my mother was born. His surviving daughters think he probably did work around the Bush Hotel in Carrick until 1911 when he went to work in the town for Arthur Guinness Son & Company, Ltd., the brewing company for which he worked until his retirement in 1950. He eventually became the superintendent of the Guinness distribution depot in Carrick. His responsibility was to keep the town's several pubs—and the ones in the surrounding districts—supplied with barrels of stout brought from the Dublin brewery by barge. It was, by Irish standards, a fearsome obligation.

When she was not looking after her children, Bridget Conlon worked at the Bush, cleaning rooms, clearing ashes from the fireplace in each room, and putting down turf and kindling for the next guests. The Bush dates from 1793, when it was built as an inn to accommodate travelers on the coach route between Dublin and Sligo. It still operates in Carrick-on-Shannon.

My mother, who sometimes accompanied her mother to the Bush, often told us that she believed it to be the most elegant place on earth. There were days, she said, when, instead of helping her mother, she would stand gazing out a second-floor window of the Bush at the town of Carrick-on-Shannon arrayed before her.

Carrick is a picturesque west Ireland town on the Shannon River in the province of Connaught, about one hundred miles northwest of Dublin. It is the administrative seat of County Leitrim, and its population, according to the 2002 census in Ireland, was 2,237, an increase of two hundred since the previous census. It is the first population gain, the locals say, since before the Famine in the 1840s. It is probably safe to say the population in 1909 was not much different than it is today.

The town's location on the river has made it a popular tourist destination, home to a thriving boating industry that rents cruisers to vacationers who want to navigate the Shannon and its waterways. Carrick has also become a weekend favorite of young Dubliners who drive two hours to party in its new clubs. Holiday homes have sprung up along the Shannon's banks, and new industry—most notably MBNA, the American credit card company, and Masonite, which manufactures high-density fiberboard products for the building industry—has brought nearly two thousand jobs to the region. Shane G. Flynn, of the Carrick-on-Shannon Flynns, the CEO of MBNA Europe, was instrumental in getting the company to locate a customer operations center there, creating nine hundred new jobs. Masonite's nearly four hundred employees make molded door facings that are exported to more than thirty European countries.

In short, the town has come a long way since its founding in 1611, when England's King James I granted the castle and lands of Carrick to a captain in his army. In 1652 Carrick and nearby Jamestown surrendered to the forces of Oliver Cromwell. They were two of the last places in Ireland to capitulate.

In the seventeenth century, and most of the eighteenth, Carrick was essentially a Protestant town. Catholics were permitted to live in a district called "The Liberty," across the Shannon, outside the borough boundary. When the Penal Laws, a series of anti-Catholic measures, were imposed in 1698, no Catholics were allowed to live anywhere in Carrick.

As a teenager my mother took it upon herself to try to bridge any gulf that might have remained between Protestants and Catholics in Carrick. She went sweet on a Protestant boy named Willie McNutt. Her father, more interested in avoiding scandal—always an abiding concern in James Conlon's life—than in encouraging any burgeoning ecumenical movement in his household, shipped Mae off to Enniskillen, about forty miles away, to live with an aunt. She was not allowed back until her father decided—incorrectly—that the romance had cooled.

It is probably reasonable to presume that when James bundled his newborn daughter in a white wool shawl that January morning and carried her to St. Mary's Church in Carrick to be baptized, the last thing on his mind was the day she would begin fancying boys. As soon as she was old enough, she was sent to the Marist Convent School in Carrick where she stayed until she reached the seventh grade. When she was twelve and getting ready to leave for school one memorable morning, her mother told her, "There'll be no more school. I need you here."

"I thought it was wonderful," my mother said whenever she talked about that day. "It's not that I hated school, but the thought of never having to go back again really appealed to me."

The only complaint I ever heard from my mother about her school years was about being forced to write with her right hand. She was left-handed, *a ciotóige* in Irish (pronounced kithogue). So whenever she took the pen in her left hand, her teacher would rap her knuckles, a painful and regular reminder to change hands. After nearly seven years of knuckle rapping, my mother was turned loose by the good sisters at the Marist Convent, a spoiled lefty unable to write legibly with either hand.

I remember my profound embarrassment on being sent to the store as a child and being asked by the neighborhood grocers to help decipher her shopping list. Al, eponymous co-owner and 50 percent of the workforce at Al's Market down the street from our house, added to my chagrin by asking me during one decryption session what my mother's nationality was, as he was convinced that English was not her first language.

When I told my mother that Al could not read her writing, she said she was not surprised, adding, "He's from Syria, isn't he?"

My brother Bill maintains that his secret for deciphering Mae Shine's writing was to look for a key word or phrase in her notes, one he could read, and use it to unlock the mystery of the remainder of the message. "I remember her using 'icebox' in a lot of her notes," Bill recalls, "as in 'supper's in the icebox,' and I was always able to work things out from there."

When Mae was fourteen, she went to work in Carrick as a housekeeper for a Miss Skinner and a short time later moved into the home of Dr. Bradshaw and his family to become part of the household staff. Bradshaw was a physician and a prominent citizen of Carrick. The Bradshaws were Protestant and lived in a large house in the part of town called St. George's Terrace. It was, my mother said, where the gentry lived. She also called it Carrick's "high-rent district." The Terrace was developed in 1824 and named after the man who owned the land, Charles Manners St. George, an Englishman who spent his summers in Carrick. The residents of St. George's Terrace included people who spent much of their time at their ancestral homes in England, making it reasonable to assume that their roots in Ireland probably could not be traced back to the ancient Gaels.

Among the people who lived in the Terrace were some who were descended from the Anglo-Irish Ascendancy, the Protestant landowning class that dominated Irish social, political, cultural, and economic life during the eighteenth and nineteenth centuries. They and their descendants lived lives of power and privilege in their grand houses and mansions, while their Irish tenants often lived in wretched poverty, struggling to pay their rents while living with the somber reality that a crop failure meant dealing with the specter of starvation.

After 1698 the Penal Laws prohibited Catholics from holding any office of state, running for Parliament, voting, or buying land. A Catholic could not hold a land lease longer than thirty-one years, and on his death the land was divided among all his children. This was to keep Catholics from accumulating large amounts of land. But if one son converted to Protestantism, the land, in its entirety, passed to him. By the 1770s it was estimated that only 5 percent of the land in Ireland remained in Catholic hands.

Farmers were also required by law to tithe, to give 10 percent of whatever they produced, livestock or crops, to the Church of England, to which virtually none of them belonged. Failure to pay meant that crops and livestock could be seized to satisfy the ministers' demands.

In his book *The Twilight of the Ascendancy,* Mark Bence-Jones notes that "most Irish country houses gave occasional sustenance to a following of people who were not beggars in that they did not actually ask for help, but turned up from time to time knowing that they would be given something if they did not come too often. Mrs. Brooke, of Summerton in County Dublin, a sister of Viscount Monck, had a large clientele of this kind. The more privileged members were allowed to tap at her sitting-room window to give notice of their arrival. She would open the window and engage in conversation which varied in length with the visitor's standing; she would then dispense a few coppers and send the visitor round to the back door for cold meat sandwiches and—if it was a lucky day—a bowl of soup. The lesser members of the clientele would sit patiently on the steps of the hall door until Mrs. Brooke came out for her morning walk, it being not done for them to ring the bell. When she emerged, they received the same treatment as those enjoying the privilege of tapping on her window. Some of the visitors sang for their supper: either literally or by regaling Mrs. Brooke with news of distant friends and relations whose houses were on their beat."

I cannot read those lines without seeing in my mind the image of my grandfather, James Conlon, his cap in his hand, his pride behind him, when he would turn up at the Bradshaws' back door, as he did each December 25, to ask for a bit of brandy sauce for his Christmas pudding.

The Ascendancy went into decline in the middle of the eighteenth century, after the British Parliament passed the Catholic Emancipation Act, which gave the Irish Catholics, among other things, the right to hold public office in Ireland. Depressed economic conditions and increasing agitation by the Irish over the ownership of land added to the decline. Despite all that, many Anglo-Irish families continued to live in the grand manner well into the twentieth century. Today some of their grand homes are offered for rental to visitors eager to step back into another time in the life of Ireland.

For two weeks in 1984, my brothers and I rented Glin Castle, an imposing Georgian manor house in County Limerick, in the small village of Glin. It is a magnificent place, an architectural wonder overlooking the Shannon River. Crenellations were added in the early 1800s, giving it an unusual Gothic look. It is still owned by the Knight of Glin, a direct descendant of the family that built it in 1780. It was filled with period furniture, rare books, fine silver and china, its walls hung with dark, somber portraits of the family that had lived there for more than two hundred years.

When we drove through the imposing gate, past the gate lodge, and up the broad avenue, my mother looked at the walls that surrounded the demesne and at the house, shining and magnificent on a small rise of land, and said quietly, "It's the symbol of everything that was ever wrong with this country."

I think now that she considered Glin Castle a reminder of the Ireland she had known as a young woman, a layered society with the privileged comfortably in place at the top and those at the bottom expected to be satisfied with whatever benefit managed to trickle down to their level. But she still appeared to enjoy her two weeks there, much of it spent in the kitchen and the scullery with the ladies who cooked and cleaned, their laughter echoing up the back stairs every night and through the high-ceilinged halls.

My mother's description of her life with the Bradshaws was an uncomplicated one. "I shopped, cleaned, answered the door, ran errands, and every afternoon put on a white apron and served tea to Mrs. Bradshaw and her lady friends," she said.

She minded the children, got them their meals, bathed them, and put them to bed after making sure they said their prayers.

My mother liked the Bradshaws. They treated her well and paid her fairly; but, though they made her feel welcome in their household, it was always clear that she was a servant. No matter how hard she tried to imagine it otherwise, it was the only life she could see ahead of her.

Seamus, my mother's youngest brother, remembers that Mrs. Bradshaw's sister was married to one of the Kirkwoods who lived in a manor house called Woodbrook, about four miles from Carrick. "They [the Kirkwoods] were good people, and we always got some toys from them for Christmas," Seamus said.

My mother's sisters, Kitty, Midge, and Gertie, remember the gifts as "secondhand toys all parceled up to look like new." It was, in a manner of speaking, the twentieth-century equivalent of tapping at Mrs. Brooke's sitting-room window.

In the midst of all that, the idea of leaving Ireland was beginning to take root. My mother said she could not remember the precise moment when she decided to leave. "But I had known for a long time that if I stayed in Carrick-on-Shannon until I died," she said, "I knew I'd never live in a house this nice and I'd never have a girl bringing me tea every afternoon and calling me 'milady.'"

In 1928, after she had been in America a year, she got a Christmas letter from Mrs. Bradshaw. It was written in pencil—for which she apologized—and on quality stationery, "Civic Bond" the watermark said, vastly superior to the inexpensive lined notebook paper used by my grandparents to write their daughter in America.

In the letter Mrs. Bradshaw wished Mae "a very happy xmas

and a glad new year" and said she was pleased to hear from the Conlons that Mae was doing well in America and liked her new work.

"I hope you will write to me and tell me all about yourself and how you are getting on," she wrote. "I shall be very interested to hear all the news. You were such a good little girl and understood what I liked so well."

It was a chatty letter. She talked about her three new cats, about Tommy McPartland's death, about Mrs. Beresford's eldest son's going off to Australia, and about the return of Miss B. from India. She reported that "our Miss Kitty" would soon be back from school and how "Master Tom" was growing so tall.

"I still miss you a lot, dear Mae," she wrote. "I don't expect you to ever come back to Ireland."

She enclosed two small linen handkerchiefs and closed by writing, "I hope you will be very lucky always. Again, with very best wishes, I am, your affectionate mistress, Ethel Bradshaw."

In spite of how Mae Conlon's circumstances might have changed, it was clear to Mrs. Bradshaw that she would always be her mistress and Mae Conlon would always be the pretty little Irish serving girl in a starched apron moving quietly on the back stairs of the house in St. George's Terrace.

Mae Conlon put the letter in the green box and never looked back.

Although most of the people in Carrick were not as rigidly status conscious as the Anglo-Irish Ascendancy, snobbery managed to manifest itself in small ways in the life of the town. When my brothers and I visited our aunts in January 2004, Kitty, Midge, and Gertie shared painful memories of being arranged by the nuns according to status at school functions such as music recitals.

Our aunts told us how the children of the merchants and the shop owners were given places in the front, the children of the laborers behind them. "We always seemed to be in the last row [for a recital]," Gertie recalled. "It had nothing to do with how clever you were, just who your family was."

"It was as if we were being robbed of our self-esteem," Midge said. "We felt like the lowest form of life."

It was clear during our visit to England that even after sixty years, the memories are still painful. "The idea that they [a certain family in Carrick] believed that they were better than we were," Kitty said, "is ridiculous." Some of the native Irish, following the pattern established by the Anglo-Irish, took it upon themselves to establish their own social hierarchy. Most were people with the aspirations but not the wherewithal to be part of the gentry. They were dismissed contemptuously as the "mock gentry," or "squireens," little squires, but it was clear from what our aunts told us that the nuns, at least, had taken the views of the squireens to heart.

Kitty, Midge, and Gertie remembered the humiliation of being sent home from school by the nuns to get the money they were supposed to have brought to school to help pay for coal to heat the classrooms, money their mother had told them that morning she did not have.

"But they sent us home anyway," Midge remembered, "even when we told them our mother didn't have the money." When they returned without it, they were scolded again in front of their classmates, their humiliation compounded.

The sisters told us of one unhappy exercise in which the children at the convent school who produced what the nuns judged to be substandard work were made to parade around the walkway outside the school with their papers pinned to their dresses, small mortifications whose pain still clung after more than sixty years.

Kitty and Midge live with their husbands in Surrey, outside London, close to their families. Kitty was born in 1924, Midge in 1925. Gertie, called Trudy by her family in England, was born in 1932, the last of the Conlon girls. She died on July 27, 2004, of complications from what was to have been a routine surgical procedure. She is buried in Chertsey Cemetery, Surrey, with her parents and sister Annie. References to her in this book will not be in the past tense. My brothers and I regard her as part of our lives, part of the present.

Whatever other social differences existed in Carrick, there was no disputing the status of the people who lived in the Terrace. My mother told us that virtually all the prominent families in Carrick-on-Shannon had servants, young girls from the town or nearby farms who worked as housekeepers and nannies while their fathers and brothers tended the grounds, kept the outbuildings in repair, and cared for the horses.

She said it was "an English thing" and never seemed to be able to come to terms with all of it, especially families that turned over to strangers, young women who were certainly not considered their social or cultural equals, the responsibility of caring for their children.

My grandfather did some work for the Bradshaws while my mother worked for them, a reason perhaps for his annual ration of brandy sauce. After Mae left for America, her brother John came to work for Mrs. Bradshaw. In a 1937 letter my grandfather seemed pleased to report to his daughter that "Joe [another brother] is in Mrs. Beresford's learning to be a house boy. She is going to train him." Mrs. Beresford, a friend of the Bradshaws, was the wife of the rector of St. George's, the Church of Ireland church in Carrick.

My mother also told us that some people of means in the area often took servants with them when they moved to places like Canada, Australia, England, or the United States or sent for them once they had settled. It was, my mother said, as if the middle- and upper-middle classes were unable to function in the world without their servants.

When Mae Conlon had enough money saved for one-way passage to America, she told her parents she was leaving. It was 1927. She was eighteen.

Her father wrote to his friend's daughter, Annie Riley, the one later said to be a brothel keeper, to ask whether she would sponsor Mae. She and her husband lived in Duluth, Minnesota. It is not clear how James Conlon knew Annie's family. What is clear is that neither he nor my grandmother, a devoted and lifelong member of the Children of Mary, had any reason to be concerned about Annie's character.

It was a puzzling circumstance to the Conlons and their friends in Carrick, Mae Conlon's going to someplace in America called Duluth in a state called Minnesota. They knew about New York, Boston, and Chicago, even Detroit, but couldn't recall ever knowing anyone from Carrick or the surrounding area who went to America and ended up in Duluth.

Annie's questionable occupation was, as best I can recall, never high on the list of things that emerged as topics of conversation during dinner at our house. It was mentioned only in passing, usually in one of those "I wonder whatever happened to" conversations about her sudden and unexplained disappearance from these shores. In fact, it was not until Uncle Seamus came to live with my mother and father in Detroit in 1958, after he was demobilized from the British army, that the whole question of Annie's livelihood received a proper airing.

Seamus described Annie's line of work simply. He said she was running a "knock-shop." My mother quietly disputed the description, admitting only that there seemed to be unusual things going on at the Rileys' house in Duluth, lots of activity she really didn't understand. She said she paid little attention to most of what was going on around her, arguing that she was "too green" and "just off the boat." She was a refugee, she explained, from a sheltered life in rural Ireland where this kind of situation, if it existed at all, was certainly never talked about. Her convenient fallback was, as often as not, the blushing innocence of the country girl, a claim we'll dispose of later. But I suppose that if she believed there were no homosexuals in Ireland, it might be safe to assume that she also believed there were no brothels in Duluth.

Now even the most proper families have their skeletons—secret drinkers, cross-dressers, kleptomaniacs—mundane failings that somehow seem more scandalous than they really are when we're busy trying to sweep them under the rug. But a madam! A brothel keeper! Now that was a skeleton to conjure with.

In the interest of fairness I should point out here that I have no independent evidence of Annie's involvement in the flesh trade. Seamus's assurance that this was indeed the situation, and my mother's failure to mount any kind of credible defense on behalf of the couple, makes for at least a limited circumstantial case, although not one that would enjoy a strong chance of success in a court of law.

But there is still the question of Annie's sudden departure. Nobody seems to quarrel with the idea that she was deported to England. The reason? "Moral turpitude," Seamus proclaimed knowingly, which indicated to me a level of awareness of the situation that somehow had not, over the years, been articulated freely in Detroit.

Annie went to England, Seamus added, because the opportunities in Ireland for success in her line of work were sorely limited. Too much amateur competition, he said and, before my mother shut him up, started to mention something about "knee-tremblers" against the outside wall of Ging Duignan's public house in Carrick.

I'm not sure if I actually remember Annie. Sometimes I think I do, but then I decide it's a memory conditioned by my parents' wedding portrait, which hung on our wall when we were kids and still claims an honored place on my own. My father, twenty years older than his bride and a somber Kerryman who had the good fortune to be born into a family with its own dairy farm and the misfortune not to be the oldest son; his younger brother, Mike, the best man, a bull-necked streetcar motorman and lifelong bachelor; and Annie, the maid of honor, tall and broad-shouldered, an enigmatic half-smile on her otherwise humorless face, standing behind Mary Ellen Shine, the flower of Carrick-on-Shannon.

Before Mae took the train from Carrick to Cobh, the seaport in Cork, the town photographer brought his camera and tripod to the Conlon house and posed her in the back garden for a final formal photograph with her family. She was wearing the outfit she would wear on the ship, her single suitcase off to the side, out of the picture. Nobody looked happy.

Months earlier the same photographer had posed her against the stone wall of the garden for the unsmiling image that was now affixed to the third page of her Irish Free State passport. It contained the visa stamp from the American consulate in Dublin that granted her permission to immigrate to the United States. She was assigned Quota Immigration Visa No. 13133. On the line requiring the description of her profession, the word *domestic* was written in blue ink.

My mother sailed to America on the SS *Republic,* a United States Lines ship. In a group picture of the passengers, taken on deck just before their arrival, she is standing at the center left of the crowd, hatless and unsmiling. She is wearing a dark sweater, the long pointed collar of her blouse on the outside. She is standing shoulder to shoulder with men with big mustaches and big caps, women with old-fashioned hats, head scarves, and shawls, some of them holding babies or large bundles, or both, all pressing to get in position so at least their faces would appear in the picture. All on the threshold of a new life, their expressions, like my mother's, offering no clue to their emotions, their thoughts as unfocused as the gray expanse of sea behind them.

My mother often talked about how excited and filled with anticipation she was as she prepared to leave Ireland. In the weeks before her departure she slept little, and, when she did, she dreamed of America and what lay in store for her. She was putting her old life behind her. Eager to begin this glorious new chapter, she fretted at how slowly the ship seemed to be moving over the ocean.

On the last night at sea, Saturday, October 7, 1927, the ship's captain, A. B. Randall, hosted a farewell dinner. The menu for the third-class passengers, found in the green box, listed a tempting array of foods, more elegant certainly than what was being served that night in the laborer's cottage on Carrick's Leitrim Road. My mother had a choice of potage à la reine, broiled halibut with sauce mousseline, prime rib of beef au jus, roast stuffed Philadelphia capon, green peas and rissole potatoes. Dessert was American ice cream and chocolate cake.

She was too excited to eat. On the back of the menu, in the place marked "Autographs," she had the people at her table sign in pencil—D. O'Keeffe, P. J. Mannion, Florence Sullivan, Celia Mannion, Tessie, Ernestine, and Mollie Gavahan—and then she went to bed. One more night, she thought, one more night before the great adventure begins.

But within days of her arrival in the fall of 1927 a new emotion—disappointment—had crowded out the old ones.

She hated it. Hated Duluth and hated America because, to her, Duluth was America, and Duluth was not what she had been expecting. "I had this vision of America," she told us. "Clean and beautiful, with nice neat houses with trees and flowers and white wooden fences and beautiful people with happy, smiling children." Like the pictures in the books she had seen.

From the windows of the train that carried her from New York to Duluth, she said, all she saw were junkyards, work sheds, coal piles, rusted car bodies, weed-choked fields, and mile after mile of drab, dark-gray wooden houses whose owners had long since given up any notion of keeping them painted against the soot and smoke that would soon have turned them gray again. Past brick warehouses and abandoned factories with broken windows and past groups of old men warming themselves around smoky bonfires.

In Duluth she lived in Annie's attic room, one floor up from the bathroom shared by all. The northeast wind off Lake Superior was relentless. She remembers being cold every day she lived there.

She cried herself to sleep that first night and all the nights of her first months there. And when she slept, she dreamed of Ireland.

"When I got up the first morning," she said, "there was ice in the water in my washbasin, and I started to cry again. If I had had enough money for fare home, I would have left that day."

She got a job as a housekeeper for a Jewish family in Duluth, a puzzling choice because she knew nothing of Judaism—apparently having left the Marist Convent School before the nuns were able to address the subject of comparative religions—and had never even known a Jew.

"I think Joe Fine might have been a Jew," she said once, "but I really don't know for sure." He was a jobber and worked at the tanyard, she said. He lived in Carrick, where the opportunity to practice his religion was, to be sure, severely limited.

Her Duluth employers were religiously observant, kept a kosher household, and insisted that my mother prepare and serve the meals properly. She decided early that this had less to do with religion than with complicating her life and increasing her workload. Separate dishes, separate pans, and separate utensils for meat and dairy were not part of a religious concept she was able to comprehend. She mixed them up, washed them together, and filched Passover candy before the occasion and let the blame fall on the children of the house when the shortage was discovered. She also took a decidedly relaxed approach to the instruction that, during the eight days of Passover, she could use none of the pots, pans, dishes, or utensils used during the rest of the year.

She blundered her way through a year with that family, violating their dietary laws while failing to demonstrate the slightest interest in acquiring even a rudimentary knowledge of Judaism. She preferred to learn, as she did, by trial and error—mostly error.

In the spring of 1928 Annie and her husband, for reasons never adequately explained, packed up and moved to Detroit. My mother came with them, got her own room in a house at 1780 Townsend on the city's East Side, and, armed with what had to be the most disingenuous letter of recommendation ever written, landed a job with yet another unsuspecting Jewish family.

Her new employers also lived on Detroit's East Side, near Gratiot and Fischer, and, like her Duluth family, also kept a kosher household and were religiously observant. And, like her Duluth family, this one also worked with her patiently, carefully explaining dietary laws. The family's patience apparently extended to her limited experience as a practitioner of the art of food preparation.

In 1985, when I was preparing a column for the *Detroit Free Press* on my mother's questionable employment history, she recalled one particular incident about her tenure with the East Side family.

"One day the father brought home a liverwurst and asked me to serve it for lunch," she said. "I had never seen liverwurst before and didn't know what to do with it, so I put it in a pot of water and boiled it."

I asked her how it turned out.

"It melted," she said.

When she lifted the lid off the pot and looked at the gray-brown glutinous concoction bubbling inside, she marveled again at the hardy stomachs of Americans who were able to eat this kind of food and still look as healthy as they did.

She took one more job in Detroit before she married my father, who was a conductor for the city's Department of Street Railways. They met while she was riding his streetcar on her way to work.

Her new employers, the Fleishers, lived at 367 Philip, on the city's southeast side, and, if my mother got the job on the strength of yet another questionable letter of recommendation, it is probably safe to assume it did not mention the melted liverwurst.

The father, Samuel Fleisher, owned and operated a department store on East Jefferson and Beniteau, and my mother worked in the Fleishers' home doing housework, cooking, and helping to care for their children. The Fleishers were also Jewish, and, despite previous employment in two Jewish homes, it soon became clear that my mother's education in the basic tenets of Judaism still contained some significant gaps.

"I was still very young [nineteen] and very green," she explained to me in 1985, "but it never occurred to me that everybody didn't celebrate Christmas." One December day in 1928, she took two of the Fleisher children, Helen and Leslie, out to buy a Christmas tree. Helen brought along her sled to help carry the tree home.

"When the parents got home that night," my mother told me, "we had the tree up and decorated." She also had purchased a crèche with Mary, Joseph, and the infant Jesus, as well as the required supporting cast of wise men, herald angels, and some shepherds with their sheep.

That night Samuel and Frieda Fleisher drove past the house

they thought was theirs but decided could not be because there was a lighted Christmas tree in the window. When Samuel, who was driving, got to the end of the block, he turned around and went back to discover that it *was* their house and there *was* a Christmas tree in the window.

"When they came into the house, they just stood there in the doorway and stared at the tree," my mother said. "If I live to be a hundred, I don't think I'll ever forget the look on Mr. Fleisher's face that night. The kids, of course, were delighted with this wonderful surprise for their mother and father. Their parents were stunned."

Mr. Fleisher took my mother into the kitchen and explained to her gently that the tree had to come down because Christmas was not celebrated in their home. The tree was removed, the children cried, and Mae Conlon went to bed that night still perplexed that not everybody in America marked the birth of Jesus with a festive tree and midnight Mass, her education in world religions advanced one more degree.

Nearly sixty years later Mae Shine had a reunion with the Fleisher children, who had read the *Free Press* column I wrote about the episode with the Christmas tree. We had brunch at a Detroit restaurant with Maryan Fleisher Abramson, the oldest, who was wrapping Christmas merchandise at her father's store when the tree was brought home; Helen Fleisher, by then Helen Zuckerman, who had pulled the tree home on her sled, and Leslie, the younger accomplice, who came with his wife, Jean. Maryan told us she remembered my mother more as a big sister than as their housekeeper. Another thing she remembered about Mae Conlon was "the devilment popping out of her eyes."

"And it's still there," she said. "She hasn't changed a bit."

My mother often worried, looking back on those days, about any damage she might have done to those families' chances of finding a measure of eternal happiness in the next life. We told her that having put up with her as patiently as they had must certainly have worked in their favor. If there is a just and merciful God, then the celestial happiness of the people who employed her is guaranteed.

We told her it was called redemptive suffering: The more you suffer on earth, the greater your rewards in heaven. She responded as she frequently did in situations where the weight of evidence prevailed against her: She told us to go to hell.

A few years ago I saw a classified ad in a California newspaper under the heading "Nanny and Me." It was directed at Jewish mothers with children in the care of others and read: "For your care-giver and child—courses in Spanish that lovingly teach your Latina nanny the customs and daily practices of Jewish culture." An idea, I decided, that probably would not have been effective for an Irish girl who did not seem particularly interested in embracing any customs and daily practices, religious or otherwise, that she judged solely on the basis of how much more work they created for her.

Because it was clear that Mae Conlon's employment in those early years did little to improve her level of Judeo-Christian enlightenment, I once asked her if her time spent cleaning houses for other people had any impact on the quality of her own housekeeping.

"Not at all," she answered. "I keep a pretty clean house, but I'm not a fanatic about it. If I don't feel like cleaning house one day, I'll wait until the next. And if I miss a few spots, I don't lose any sleep over it."

Underscoring her relaxed approach to the domestic arts is my brother Bill's memory of coming home from high school one afternoon and finding my mother on her knees in the front room, leaning on one of the overstuffed chairs, hands clasped prayerfully.

She was not praying.

It turned out that the weekly block rosary, attended by a dozen or more neighbors, was to be held in our house that evening. My mother explained to Bill that she was checking what could be seen from a kneeling position so she would know where she had to dust.

James Conlon

I always believed that my mother's preoccupation with otherwise innocent boy-girl friendships as "occasions of sin" could be traced straight back to her father.

James Conlon was, by every account, a stern disciplinarian who set the rules for his family and expected them to be obeyed. He was not without some standing among the residents of Carrick-on-Shannon, a circumstance not surprising for the man who ran the depot that kept them supplied with Guinness stout. He was determined to protect his reputation from the slightest hint of scandal, something that was, to him, worse than death.

In World War I he had served with distinction in France with the Connaught Rangers, a legendary Irish regiment of the British army once commanded by the Duke of Wellington. James had enlisted in the Rangers in February 1903, riding up to Boyle, in nearby County Roscommon, where the regiment was headquartered. He had spent three years on active duty and was assigned to the reserve for nine years. He married Bridget Downs in Carrick on January 7, 1908. Mary Ellen, their first daughter, was born the following year.

He was recalled to duty in 1914 at the beginning of the war and served until 1918. He was part of the British Expeditionary Force in France and was assigned to the Royal Army Medical Corps. He told me when I visited him in 1954 that other Rangers claimed that the corps' acronym, RAMC, stood for "rob all my comrades," convinced that the medics made a habit of helping themselves to the belongings of the sick and wounded.

This seemed to reinforce what I have heard over the years, that members of the Connaught Rangers were "accomplished bandits" who took to heart the notion that to the victors belong the spoils. Part of the legend maintains that whenever the regiment approached a town in Ireland, a cry went up: "Mother, mother, take in the washing—the Rangers are here!"

This may be an unwarranted slur on a regiment with a proud history of service to the British Empire, but another story, this one involving the Duke of Wellington, hints that there might have been some truth to the legend.

Following an engagement during the Peninsular War (1807–14), a major conflict of the Napoleonic Wars, the duke, the regiment's commanding officer, saw a private walking off with a small pig. The duke, who had strictly forbidden plundering by his troops, confronted the soldier.

"Private," he demanded sharply, "what are you doing with that pig?"

Without hesitation the young Irish soldier, pig still firmly in his grasp, stood smartly to attention and answered: "Trying to find its mother, sir."

The story goes on to say that the duke had the man promoted to sergeant on the spot for his "brilliant defense of an indefensible position."

After World War I, James Conlon returned to Carrick and work at the Guinness depot. He also became a member of the Carrick-on-Shannon Brass and Reed Band. According to Seamus, my mother's brother, the band's most important engagements seemed to be local funerals and the annual Carrick-on-Shannon Regatta.

James played the cornet and, Seamus said, "Frank Conlon, James's brother, played the triangle, Paddy Gill played the clarinet, and 'Yankee' McGowan was the bandleader. He [McGowan] had spent about four or five months in America, and when he came back to Ireland his friends in Carrick called him 'Yankee' until the day he died.

"If they didn't get too much of the black stuff before the funeral—I'm talking about the Guinness—they would assemble and play the 'Dead March from Saul' and march through the town and out to the cemetery with the coffin," Seamus said.

"But their big outing was the Carrick-on-Shannon Regatta," he said. "First Monday in August. It was a big thing, and people used to come from all over Ireland to row down the Shannon. They built a bandstand across the Shannon next to Ging Duignan's public house, and these guys [the band members] must have had to use the toilet a lot because they kept running in and out of Ging Duignan's. By the time the bloody regatta was finished, the band had dwindled down to maybe the triangle player and the drummer."

Uncle Frank Conlon also is part of family legend for his creative effort to keep his wife, Aunt Susan, from making herself a cup of tea while he was at work. He was a notorious cheapskate, Seamus said, and it pained him to think of his wife at home "wasting" tea.

"So every morning he'd catch a live fly and put it in the bloody tea tin," Seamus said. "If Aunt Susan took the top off the tin, the fly would get out, and Frank would know she had been dipping into the tea, and all hell would break loose."

When World War II ended in 1945, Mae began entertaining thoughts of returning to Carrick to visit her parents. There were casual references to it at first and then more serious discussions, including the fare, a subject that she always concluded with, "But that's an awful lot of money." She set up potential roadblocks to the trip and, just as quickly, knocked them down. It was soon clear to her sons that she was going to go.

My mother returned to Ireland in 1949, her first visit since she had left twenty-two years earlier. I had just finished my freshman year at the University of Detroit, and Jim was a seminarian with the Carmelite Fathers in Niagara Falls, Ontario. Bill, twelve, went with her.

She found that her father's attitudes had not softened in the years she had been gone. When she told her parents one day during the visit that she was going to a dance that evening with two of her unmarried sisters—Annie and Gertie—and some of her childhood friends, her father told her he would not allow her to go. He had learned that among those who would be at the dance was Georgie Graham, a bachelor from Carrick, who apparently had been something more than just a childhood friend of my mother's. It wouldn't look right, her father said, her being a married woman and all. People will talk. Besides, he said, she needed to be home because the family said the rosary together each evening.

My mother told him that she did not need his permission to go anywhere. She was forty years old and she would damn well go to the dance if she wanted to. She didn't care how it looked, she said, and she didn't care if people talked. She also told him not to worry about her missing the rosary. She'd say it on her own—if she felt like it.

She went to the dance and had a wonderful time. It was held in the town hall in Carrick, and her younger sister, Gertie, who was seventeen at the time, remembered it as her first dance. "I wasn't allowed to wear lipstick, and Mae took me to Evelyn's [Evelyn was married to Mae's brother John; they lived in Carrick], gave me her lipstick, and I put it on before the dance and wiped it off on the way home."

When they got home that night, laughing all the way up the Priest Lane, Gertie recalled, they were unable to get into the house. Their father had locked them out. Gertie remembered climbing through a window to unlock the door. Gertie and Annie knew enough about life with James to make sure one of them lifted the hinged board on the bottom of the door that was lowered on cold days to keep the wind from blowing in. Since it was the middle of summer my mother knew her father had lowered the board, which scraped noisily on the floor when the door was opened, so he would know what time they had gotten home. Whether she ever made up the missed rosary was never determined.

A word about my brother Jim and the road to the priesthood. My father, like a lot of the Irish, considered it an unparalleled honor to have a son or daughter choose the religious life. Many believed that the parents of a priest or nun gained automatic admission to the Kingdom of Heaven when they died, no preliminary stops, no questions asked. This kind of celestial guarantee appealed to my father. Also, two of his brothers in Ireland had been Presentation Brothers.

When I was in the eighth or ninth grade, I was helping my father dig in the vegetable garden in our yard on Lycaste. As we turned over the hard dirt and broke down the clumps to make the ground more accepting of our tomato plants, my father said to me: "Well, Neal, are you thinking about going to the monks?" That was his way of inquiring about any interest I might have had in becoming a priest.

I just kept digging. What little I knew about celibacy at that point was enough for me to understand that it was not a lifestyle that appealed to me. He turned a few more shovels of dirt and said, almost to himself, "Sure and you'd rather go to the devil," which he pronounced *divil*. Not quite true, but close enough.

He turned his attention to Jim, who always seemed a better candidate for Holy Orders than either Bill or I. Jim spent a lot of time in our basement with an old lace curtain tied around his shoulders, saying make-believe Masses and passing out Necco candy wafers at "communion," a circumstance that always guaranteed an impressive turnout of neighborhood kids at his liturgies.

When he finished the eighth grade at St. Rose, Jim entered the Carmelite Fathers' seminary and stayed through his high school years but decided not to continue his priestly studies. My mother was secretly pleased, my father clearly disappointed. Jim came back to Detroit and was drafted into the army. He spent two years in the service, and after his discharge he graduated from the University of Detroit and got a law degree from the Detroit College of Law.

If Pat Shine ever mourned the loss of his guaranteed ticket to heaven, he never mentioned it. Nor did he ever ask if fathers of lawyers got any special consideration on Judgment Day. I think he already knew the answer to that question.

Because my mother mentioned it often, usually only in passing, we were aware of the importance of prayer—particularly the rosary—in the life of the Conlons in Carrick. As for the Shines of Detroit, there was never any communal prayer. We prayed in church, and my mother and father apparently considered that a sufficient display of piety.

In the 1950s the idea of people in the same neighborhood saying the rosary at a different house each week took hold in Detroit. Although my mother readily offered our house as a prayer site, she never seemed especially enthusiastic about it, worrying more about what desserts she would serve for the post-rosary social gathering than about the rosary itself.

It wasn't until my mother's brother Seamus came to live with us in 1958 that we were exposed to a harsher view of James Conlon's preoccupation with family prayer. Seamus was born in 1920 and remembers growing up in Carrick as a not unpleasant experience.

"We had a very, very good life in Carrick," he told my brother Jim in 1995. "My father was working at Guinness's. He was getting about three pound-ten [shillings] a week. That would be about $19 a week. We always had enough to eat, but we were brought up in a very, very rigid and domineering environment. My father was strict, much more so than he should have been.

"He was a good man. I have nothing to say against James Conlon. He was a damned good man. He brought up a big family. But what he said was the law. And there were certain rules you had to follow in that house, and if you broke the rules you were in trouble."

One of those rules was that the family said the rosary together every night. Every member of the family had to be there at 7 p.m., ready to pray. No excuses, no exemptions, certainly not for dances.

Kitty, Midge, and Gertie recalled that if you feigned sickness to avoid the rosary, you were required to say the prayers from bed—and do it loud enough to be heard in the parlor.

My brother Bill remembers that during his visit to Carrick with Ma in 1949, he found the rosary ritual tedious. He was twelve and would rather have been outside with the neighborhood children than on his knees reciting the rosary inside 4 Kingston Terrace. "So I would always be sure to find a place to kneel where I could look out the window to see what was going on outside. It helped pass the time."

Once a month, Seamus said, James also led them in prayers in which the family reconsecrated itself to the Sacred Heart of Jesus. It was called the "Holy Hour." The Conlons gathered those evenings in front of the statue of the Sacred Heart, a small votive candle flickering in its red glass holder, and prayed for the members of the family who had left Ireland, including Mae and her brother Michael, who came to Detroit in 1928.

"That was the rosary you really tried to avoid if you could get away with it for any reason because it really stretched it out," Seamus said. "It was all for our good, but it didn't do any good, really. The object was to get away from Ireland, forget the rosary, forget Mass, forget your religion. 'I don't want any more of this that's been beaten into me from the time I was seven.' And it was a shame to be brought up in an environment like that because it scarred young Irish people like me, and my brothers and sisters, for the rest of our lives. When any of the Conlons reached the age when they could strike out on their own, they couldn't get away quick enough."

Seamus left school at fourteen and went to work. A short time later he joined three of his brothers in England and found work as a laborer. When World War II started, he joined the British army and stayed in for twenty years. After he moved to Detroit, he took correspondence courses in accounting, overcame alcoholism, married, and moved to California, where he managed a chain of supermarkets near San Diego. He died in California in 2000.

I met my grandparents for the first time in 1954. I was in the army, stationed in Salzburg, Austria. I caught a free ride on a U.S.

Air Force plane to London and took the train to Holyhead, Wales, and the ferry across to Dun Laoghaire. I took a train to Carrick, where Bridget and James met me at the station with a hired car driven by Joe Stanford, the Carrick taxi driver. After he drove us to the house on Kingston Terrace, he parked his black Ford in front of the house and joined us for tea in the Conlon kitchen to help celebrate my arrival.

I was the first grandchild, and my grandmother fussed over me from the moment I stepped off the train until the day I left. To every person we met in Carrick she said, "It's Mae's boy. Isn't he the grand big lad?" She asked me if all the men in America were as big as I was. I was six-one and told her the country was full of people taller than I, something she had trouble believing.

James was cordial but reserved. More formal, I thought, than I had expected my grandfather would be. While it is true that I had no experience as a grandson—my father's parents died in Ireland in the 1930s—my expectations included something a little less formal than a brief handshake. I suppose if I had considered it all in terms of my own father's apparent reluctance to respond warmly or with affection to his sons—I cannot remember a hug or kiss from him—I might have been able to look at it all as a kind of natural reluctance by Irish men, or simply men of that generation, who seemed to believe anything that might be taken for an expression of emotional attachment was something to be avoided. Maybe it's one of the reasons I kiss all my children, including the boys, whenever I see them.

When my grandfather met me at the station, he was wearing a gray gabardine overcoat that had been mine when I was in high school. My mother, operating on the doctrine of waste not, want not, a dominant principle in her life, had sent it to him. It was too big for him. He was five-eight and the coat was too long, too large in the shoulders, and the sleeves nearly covered his hands. I looked at him standing on the platform of the Carrick station and thought that this was surely one time when "Don't worry, he'll grow into it," my mother's universal pronouncement in the face of oversized apparel or footwear, would have been unconvincing.

James Conlon had retired from Guinness three years earlier, and his daughter Annie was still living at home. He walked me through the town that first day, making sure we visited all the pubs. He was greeted warmly by the publicans, only fitting for the man who had been the dependable purveyor of their most important product for nearly half a century.

As he did on most of our subsequent walks, he took me to the old Guinness depot at the foot of Bridge Street, next to the Shannon, next to the massive 1846 stone bridge that crossed into Roscommon. The depot was closed by this time, and he posed sadly in front of the empty building, standing solemnly before the big green door, his hands pushed deep into the pockets of the oversized gabardine overcoat from America, as he looked out at the river. Whatever thoughts might have crowded his mind on those mornings, he never shared any with me. After a few minutes he would turn away from the river and start up the stone steps to Bridge Street.

As we walked through the town, he would point to this building or that business, talking about how long the Lowes had owned and operated the pub or how many years the Costellos had been in the grocery business; about who lived where and how many generations of their family lived there before them. To him the past was a comfortable refuge, and he believed the present should be no more than a reflection of that past, durable and unchanging.

As we walked, men tipped their hats to him or tugged the bill of their caps when we passed and said, "Fine day, James." And he would respond, "Fine day, indeed, thank God."

It became clear to me during my visit that station was important to him. When he introduced me to people we met on our walk, he took care when they had left to brief me on their pedigree, telling me what kind of work they did, what kind of families they had come from, and their relative standing in the social hierarchy of Carrick-on-Shannon. My mother had told me over the years that appearances were as important to him as anything else in his life and that he feared scandal above all other earthly torments.

Remember, this was the man who had sent his oldest daughter to live with an aunt in another town because of her friendship with a Protestant boy. My mother told us, years after the fact, that she had resumed her friendship with Willie McNutt when she got back from Enniskillen, knowing full well that her life was at far greater risk than her soul if her father ever found out.

At the time of my first visit, Annie, the second youngest of the Conlon girls, was twenty-four, a few months older than I was. She became my personal guide to the delights of Carrick-on-Shannon. She was a happy young woman with red cheeks and a bright smile who laughed a lot. She seemed as amused at having a nephew only five months younger than she was as I was at having an aunt nearly my age. She told me all she could about Carrick and its people. In 1954 she was working for the Gorman family, caring for their children. The Gormans were drapers (they sold cloth) and had a shop in Carrick. She worked for other families in Carrick and, as a result, was privy to their secrets, which she shared freely with me, something she felt comfortable doing since I was only passing through.

She told me, for example, that some of the people in Carrick wouldn't buy their milk from Bridget McGreevy because she let her cows graze in the cemetery, feeding on grass that was being nourished, so to speak, by their deceased ancestors. I went with Annie a few times to pick up a can of milk from Mrs. McGreevy for the tea or the stirabout, a porridge into which the milk was stirred. When I did, I was always concerned less with the provenance of her cows' diet than with the real possibility that the long, gray ash that hung from the Woodbine she always had tucked in one corner of her mouth would end up in the milk. According to Annie, it was a minor calamity that occurred every so often but that apparently posed no serious health risk to consumers. More troubling, Annie said, were the errant hairs that occasionally found their way into the milk and had to be fished out before it was used.

The best way to avoid ashes in the milk, Annie said, was not to say anything to Mrs. McGreevy that required a reply while she was separating the milk. Two-way conversation, Annie said, inevitably triggered falling ash. Annie also told me that "contamination" was probably too strong a word and assured me that no one had ever fallen ill from drinking Mrs. McGreevy's milk.

For every question Annie answered on our journeys through Carrick, she asked five. What was America like? Was it nicer than Ireland? Had I ever been to New York or Hollywood? Was Chicago really full of gangsters? Did I think she'd like America? It was clear that even though she was curious about the world beyond Carrick-on-Shannon, it probably would never be part of her life.

Another person who made sure I saw everything that was important in the town was Pat Dunne, proprietor, editor, and, it appeared, chief reporter of the *Leitrim Observer,* Carrick's weekly newspaper. He was pleased, he told me, to be able to entertain "an American journalist," a designation to which I certainly aspired but to which I was not yet really entitled. I did not tell him I was just a copyboy at the *Detroit Free Press,* letting him assume for the moment that I was, indeed, an American journalist.

One morning he took me with him on his news-gathering rounds, dropping in on various merchants and solicitors, chatting with people on the street, and putting it all down in his notebook. He kept his head canted uncomfortably to one side to keep the starched collar of his shirt from rubbing against an angry red carbuncle on the back of his neck. My grandmother later explained that "poor Pat" suffered from an affliction she called "the pox."

Our first stop had been the courthouse, obviously the *Observer*'s most important source of news. In court that morning John Joseph Doherty was charged by an inspector from the Ministry of Agriculture with being in possession of an unlicensed black polly bull. Doherty swore the bull was only seven months and not yet old enough to require a license. The inspector, James Maloney, said the bull was at least fifteen months old, basing his estimate on his seven years' experience as an inspector and as someone who "was born on a farm and of farming stock." After weighing testimony from both men, District Justice D. O'Donachadha ruled that because there was some doubt as to the actual age of the bull, Doherty was entitled to the benefit of the doubt and dismissed the case. After Patrick Geraghty was fined for having his pub open at 2 a.m., well after the legal closing time, we left. Pat Dunne went back to the *Observer* to write his stories, and I went back to the Conlons', eager to relate the story of the unlicensed polly bull of indeterminate age.

I was singularly impressed that morning by the willingness of Justice O'Donachadha to believe the testimony of defendants in several cases for reasons no more compelling than that they had sworn a sacred oath to tell the truth and, he believed, certainly would not perjure themselves. Years later, on more than one occasion, I sat at the press table in Detroit's Recorder's Court listening to highly questionable testimony from defendants who had also sworn to be truthful. I decided that every lawbreaker in the room would have seen Justice O'Donachadha as a gift from judicial heaven.

In the next edition of the *Leitrim Observer,* Dunne took note of my visit to Carrick. On page five, under the heading "Carrick-on-Shannon News," and hammocked between items announcing the appointment of Rev. Father McCauley as the new assistant curate in Carrick and the visit to the town by T. F. O'Higgins, Ireland's minister for health, Dunne wrote: "Mr. Neil [*sic*] Shine, Detroit, son of Mr. Patrick Shine and Mrs. Mae Shine (nee Conlon) who has been serving with the U.S.A. forces in Salsburg [*sic*], Australia [*sic*], is on a visit to his grandparents, Mr. and Mrs. James Conlon, Kingston Terrace, Carrick-on-Shannon."

The item was not without a few small mistakes, and certainly not nearly as interesting as the controversy involving Mr. Doherty's bull, but my grandparents thought it was wonderful, and I still have the copy I took away from Carrick. It was my first international press notice.

During my stay in Carrick I told Annie and my grandparents that I would be stopping in Paris for four days on my way back to Salzburg. A few days before I was to leave, Annie asked me what Paris was like. I told her I had never been to Paris, but I was sure it was not like Carrick or even Dublin. She asked me if I thought she'd ever be able to see Paris. I told her all things were possible. Then I said that if she really wanted to see Paris, I would take her with me. I told her she had been gracious enough to show me Carrick-on-Shannon. Now we could experience Paris together.

Her initial excitement passed quickly. "He'll never let me go," she said quietly.

I talked to her father that night. I told him I had enough money to pay her airfare and for the accommodations in Paris. The hotel where I had reservations near the Place de l'Opéra was inexpensive but very nice. She would have her own room, and on Monday I would put her on the plane to Dublin, and she could take the train back to Carrick. He looked at me for a moment without speaking. Then he said he couldn't let her go.

I asked him why. "You have a wife and child in America," he answered, surprised that I even had to ask.

"She's my aunt," I said. "Would you feel better if I called my wife so she can tell you she has no problem with my taking Annie to Paris?" He said that wasn't the point. It was the appearance of it all. It wouldn't look right, Annie's going off to Paris with a married man, even if he was her nephew. People would talk. James Conlon could live with a lot of things; people talking was not one of them.

Annie cried a little when I told her. She said she tried to expect the worst and not hope for the best, but she couldn't help it. Then she smiled and told me that she thought that James's perception of Paris as a sinful place had as much to do with his decision as my status as a married nephew. He worried a lot about sin, she said.

When the Gaiety Cinema opened in Carrick in 1933, she told me, James was not pleased and predicted that nothing good would come of it. He may even have seen it as Carrick's first step on the road to becoming another Paris, she said. I told Annie that maybe I should have told him I was taking her to Rome. We both laughed. It was the only light moment of the day.

The next day my grandmother took me to the Carrick cemetery on the Jamestown road to pick shamrocks. It was the best place to find them, she said, and told me it was where she got the ones she sent to us in America every St. Patrick's Day. I remembered that the shamrocks always seemed to arrive in Detroit sometime in late March or early April and fell brown and brittle from the envelope. My mother gamely floated them in a water-filled jelly glass on the kitchen windowsill, hoping they might revive. They never did.

It was raining that morning, and as we stepped carefully around the obstacles left by Mrs. McGreevy's cows, my grandmother told me not to think harshly of my grandfather. I knew Annie must have told her about Paris. "It's just his way," my grandmother said without looking up. But he was, for all that, she said, still a good man.

I left Carrick a few days later, my suitcase carried to the station not in Joe Stanford's Ford but by Tommy (Tommy the Glazier) McDermott's horse cart. I saw my grandparents one more time before the army sent me home, and I later calculated my total exposure to the only set of grandparents I had ever known at twenty-two days.

I went to Paris alone, and at each grand monument, in each museum, in each small bistro, I thought about how much Annie would have loved it. When I got back to Salzburg, I wrote and thanked her for being such a gracious guide when I was in Carrick. I told her that I sat on a bench overlooking the Seine one afternoon and that, while it was not the Shannon, it did have its own special charm. She wrote back that she saw the Shannon every day and would love to see the Seine just once.

When James and Bridget moved to a town outside London later that year to be closer to the rest of their children, Annie moved with them. She eventually married and had four children. It would be a serious understatement to say that her marriage was not the happiest circumstance in her life. We visited her several times in England over the years, and her capacity for laughter never diminished.

When she and my grandparents moved, they left the house in Kingston Terrace, the one given to my grandfather rent-free by the British army for his service with the Connaught Rangers. He told me he had expected to live out his days in that house and die in the town in which he had been born.

If England was never part of his plan, Bridget had other ideas. Her life with James Conlon was not notable for the number of times she got her way with him, but she was determined to live near her children.

During my visit that autumn she had been busy getting ready for the move. I watched as she decided what they would take and what she would give away. She gave Tessie Carr two bedspreads. Hannah Doyle asked for, and was given, "the blue dishes," the ones she said she'd always liked. Josie Haney came for tea one afternoon and left with a large serving dish.

While I sat in the front room trying, with little success, to make conversation with my grandfather, Bridget Conlon fussed happily in the kitchen, where I could hear her singing bits of the popular American song "The Naughty Lady of Shady Lane." James Conlon's lifelong friend Packy Graham came by one afternoon to chat but left when it seemed clear that James was in no mood for small talk.

I saw my grandparents the following February in England. They were living with their son Brian and his family, and James was no more or no less talkative than he had been in Carrick five months earlier. But he seemed older, a bit slower, with a slope to his shoulders that I had not noticed before, like a man who had lost something important.

The day I left England we took pictures in Brian's back garden. I hugged my grandmother and kissed her good-bye and shook hands with my grandfather, who said nothing. I knew it would be the last time I would ever see them.

James Conlon died in 1958, Bridget three years later. Annie, who never managed to get to Paris, was sixty-nine when she died in England in 1999. She is buried in the Chertsey Cemetery in Surrey, near her mother and father. No shamrocks grow there, and it is far from the quiet Carrick cemetery out the Jamestown road.

In Carrick-on-Shannon the Gaiety is still screening movies more than seventy years after it opened, and there is no clear evidence that Carrick is any closer to being another Paris than it has ever been.

My mother never spoke much about life with her father. Stories of her childhood were not part of our lives. Perhaps it is because she never had a childhood to speak of. Out of school at twelve to work at home—or at the Bush Hotel with her mother—and then off to the Bradshaws' at fourteen as a servant.

But in the long letters James sent her, there is a warmth and affection in which he apparently did not indulge when she was close enough for him to express those thoughts in person or to put his arms around her. He wrote that he was asking God to "guide and guard you as you are the best little girl in all the world. God bless you." They were always signed, "I remain, as ever, your loving Daddy," or "Your affectionate Daddy," and were always followed by a half-dozen or so X's put there by the siblings she left behind.

On April 16, 1929, after her parents received a letter from my mother telling them that she was going to be married, her mother wrote a poignant letter to her first child: "I hope you have the best of luck and may God bless you both as I could say nothing else to you as you were the best girl a mother ever reared, but I feel as if I am losing you now but I know you won't forget us."

Tempering the sadness was Bridget Conlon's realization that her daughter was putting behind her a life as a domestic, as a servant. "It was a great surprise to me," she wrote, "and when I read it I felt sorry but I still felt glad as it is a poor thing to be all your life working for strangers." It was signed "Mammy."

Every time I read this letter, I picture my mother walking through the town for the last time, carrying her small suitcase, stopping at the church where she had been baptized only eighteen years earlier, asking God to protect her on her journey and to keep her safe in the new land, trying without success to hold back the tears by thinking about the wonderful new life that awaited her in this magic place called America.

I think about that day, about her leaving, whenever I read this poem written by Michael J. MacManus, a journalist and poet who was born in Carrick-on-Shannon in 1888:

Nothing shall be the same again
Bright birds that sing and flash a rainbow coloured wing
In Hedgerows wet with April rain and every lovely thing
Shall be less beautiful, since she, who was more
Beautiful than these, has taken wing
And flown away beyond the silent seas.

It appears from the letters that in 1937 my mother, now ten years beyond the silent seas, held out the hope of a visit to Ireland. It is difficult, years later, to imagine how she would have managed it, but her father was joyful at the prospect: "We are longing for this year to go until we see you all. I hope in God you will all be able to come home. It will be the joy of our hearts to see you."

In case she was inclined to forget, he mixed this flow of uncharacteristic affection with reminders that not much else had changed. "I must close now," he wrote in that 1937 letter, "as it is coming near rosary time. We have the Holy Hour tonight."

The only stories I can remember about my mother's life as a little girl are about the time she tried to jump across Costello's Drain, a drainage ditch in a field near her house and fell into the water, and about her earnest childhood desire to live the carefree existence of a chicken. On her way to school she would sometimes stop to watch the chickens in the neighbors' gardens, deciding that the birds had a pretty good life: always enough food and water, no housework or schoolwork, no rapped knuckles, no scolding by the sisters for saying "me bag" instead of "my bag," no worldly responsibilities.

She told us about the time she was with a boy under one of the arches of the old stone bridge over the Shannon that connected Carrick with Roscommon. Her father walked by and looked her way. Terrified, she waited until he passed, and then, at a full run, she struck out for home across the fields, over the fences, through the back gardens to her house, where she grabbed a book and sat in front of the fire.

When her father came into the house moments later and began to question her, she was so short of breath she could not answer. He asked her how long she had been home. Her mother, sensing imminent disaster, answered for her. "All afternoon," she lied. James Conlon looked at his daughter for several minutes and then left the room. My mother said that during those minutes, her life, as brief as it was, had flashed before her.

We have decided since that the boy she was with that day, whose name she never told us, was Willie McNutt, the Protestant. We also believe it probably happened after she had returned from exile in Enniskillen and had quickly—but more carefully—resumed the relationship.

Occasions of Sin

In 1938, when I was eight years old, we moved from the rented house on Beniteau to a rented upstairs flat at 1532 Lycaste. It was the first house north of Jefferson and, by prevailing neighborhood standards, no better or worse than the other houses on the street. It was frame, in need of painting, but comfortable enough with three small bedrooms, one bath, a large kitchen, a nice dining room, and a front room.

My mother made it clear shortly after the move that most of the responsibility for keeping the place clean would, not surprisingly, fall to her children. This included at least one midweek "Irish mopping" of the kitchen floor. This was an improvised cleaning process she devised and named: Splash a little water from the kettle on the middle of the linoleum floor, take a couple of swipes at it with a mop, and say, "There, that looks better." It is a tradition that, two generations later, still enjoys wide acceptance in the extended family.

Her absence of enthusiasm for housework never applied to the standards she set for her three sons. When we reached the age—which seemed terribly early to us—at which we were expected to assume the bulk of the responsibility for keeping the house clean, she demanded rigid adherence to the suddenly elevated levels of quality she had established.

We seemed to spend an inordinate amount of our Saturdays

cleaning house. Perhaps that was because we spent so much time arguing among ourselves about the fair allocation of chores. What seem now like ridiculous squabbles were perfectly reasonable to kids attempting to make sure the process was kept equitable.

Our upstairs flat on Lycaste on Detroit's East Side, where we lived from 1938 until 1948, had a very large kitchen, and that meant we had a very large floor to scrub. The linoleum had a pattern of four-by-four-inch squares. Each Saturday the two of us assigned to scrub it would count the squares, parcel them out evenly, and scrub only those squares for which we were responsible, including one half of the odd square in the corner near the icebox that was always left over when the counting was done.

Jim and I shared a bed, which we were expected to make together each morning. On some days when I was off doing something else, Jim would make the bed himself and then carefully unmake my half, pulling up the blankets, sheets, and bedspread, because he was required to make only his half.

Other chores included polishing the huge oak table and the intricately carved buffet and china cabinet in the dining room. We often cursed the faint-hearted Crowley, Milner & Company driver who came to repossess the dining room furniture years earlier but left without it. We also cursed the circumstance that thrust us into a family without sisters.

The house was on the east side of Lycaste and next to an alley. As a result, our dining room and kitchen overlooked the back of the Jefferson Inn, a thriving neighborhood bar whose clientele consisted mostly of young men from Appalachia who had come north to make their fortune in the auto plants, engaged after 1942 in the around-the-clock production of war materiel.

The Jefferson Inn's business plan was uncomplicated: to relieve these men of as much of their earnings as efficiently and as quickly as possible. The bar carried the usual selection of alcoholic offerings, along with an array of live country-western music, bad singers, and marginally entertaining floor shows. Among the stars I remember was Ferdinand the Bull, a huge (to us) animal with a shiny black coat. The bull was famed for his performance in the Tyrone Power bullfighting movie, *Blood and Sand*. I have no idea what the bull did onstage to entertain the customers of the Jefferson Inn. But when Ferdinand's handler brought him out the back door every afternoon before the show to let him poop in the parking lot of the adjacent Hudson Hotel, an enthusiastic crowd of neighborhood kids was always on hand.

You have to understand that even with the myriad of strange and quirky happenings in that East Side neighborhood, a famous Hollywood bull pooping in a parking lot qualified as something remarkably special. The handler, a friendly man with a cowboy hat, always let each of us rub Ferdinand's massive head before he took the bull back into the bar.

The only other entertainers I remember clearly were the Hilton sisters, Violet and Daisy, conjoined twins, known then as Siamese twins. They called their act "The Hilton Sisters' Revue," and the women did a song-and-dance routine and played piano, violin, saxophone, and clarinet. Between performances they often stepped into the alley to enjoy a breath of fresh air. We were always waiting. They were genuinely cordial to us, standing arm in arm, smiling sweetly, and answering our dumb questions. "Do you have to wear special dresses?" "Who gets to decide which one you'll wear?" "What do you do if your sister gets bossy?" "What if you want to get up early and your sister wants to stay in bed?"

We decided we liked them a lot. My mother, for her part, did not like them. She was reluctant to let her children consort with the Jefferson Inn's entertainers, all of whom eventually seemed to find their way to the alley. She never said as much, but I think she believed that the kind of people who performed in saloons were unsavory types and potential corrupting influences. Whenever she spotted us in the alley talking to any of them, she opened a window and called us inside, where we were told not to be talking to "those people." The truth was that "those people" provided us with a glimpse into an entirely different and fascinating world, places beyond the narrow confines of that neighborhood, and we continued to talk to them every chance we got.

The Hilton sisters had played the vaudeville circuit in cities all over the country. We were predictably impressed by the number of places they had been. My brothers and I had been to Pittsburgh. Although the Hilton sisters were a year older than our mother (we asked), they looked younger. And prettier. We decided it must have been the makeup and never mentioned it to Ma.

Another reason for Ma's concern may have been her not being on good terms with the owner of the Jefferson Inn. For one thing, the bar was, if nothing else, a noisy place. While the downtown movie theaters bragged on canvas banners hanging from their marquees that they were "COOLED BY REFRIGERATION," the message delivered in frosty blue letters with painted icicles hanging from them, refrigeration technology had yet to extend to neighborhood bars. Because of that the back door to the Jefferson Inn was always propped open to catch whatever breeze might be drifting through the alley.

The inevitable result was that the amplified sounds of the southern troubadours rolled noisily through our house on summer nights. The bar's limited restroom facilities meant that a number of the patrons, mostly (but not exclusively) men, came out to the alley to relieve themselves. And it was not unusual to get up in the morning to find one of the Jefferson Inn's customers from the previous night lying spread-eagled in our backyard. One of us was always sent down to see if the person in the yard was alive so my mother could accurately report his condition when she called the police. None was ever dead.

I don't remember being troubled by our proximity to what passed for a fleshpot in that neighborhood, and I don't think my brothers were, either. The music never kept us awake, and if the patrons were being entertained in the bar, we were being entertained in the alley by the same performers without having to pay the cover charge. Also, there were always a lot of good fights to watch because disagreements that began inside the Jefferson Inn were, with some physical assistance by the bar's bouncers, inevitably concluded in the alley under our windows.

Fighting seemed to us to be a natural by-product of drinking and amounted to a cultural fact of life in the bars along Jefferson. It was unusual to walk a dozen blocks along Jefferson on a Friday or Saturday night without seeing a fight or two. We were watching the day that Tom Dallas, the neighborhood iceman, died when his head hit the sidewalk outside the Union Bar on the corner of Jefferson and Lycaste. He was not a participant in the fight but was trying to break it up when he got knocked down. The life lesson I took home with me that day—and retain—is that insinuating yourself into a physical dispute in whose outcome you have no real stake comes with its own special dangers.

I remember clearly that the two men who had been fighting stopped when Dallas went down. Then they went back into the bar together to wait for the police and, more likely than not, to have a drink together while they waited.

This was also a time when television's Friday-night fights played to overflow crowds in the local bars (the show, *Gillette Cavalcade of Sports*, aired nationally from 1946 to 1960). My father told us that one neighborhood bar without a television set tried to compete by putting a hand-lettered sign in its window that announced, "WE DON'T HAVE TELEVISION BUT THERE'S A FIGHT HERE EVERY NIGHT."

My mother decided that in addition to being a corrupting influence on her children, the Jefferson Inn was a neighborhood nuisance. She went to the bar one afternoon to ask the owner if he would please keep the back door closed, turn down the speakers, and keep the patrons from using the alley as a toilet.

She came home from the meeting furious. She said the owner told her he was operating a licensed and legitimate business and if she was not happy with any of that, then she should consider moving. Then he dismissed her with a wave of his hand, telling her he had work to do. As young as we were—I was thirteen at the time—my brothers and I could have told the owner he was making a grievous mistake by dismissing Mae Shine, even if he had not included the gratuitous wave of the hand.

Her crusade began in earnest the next day. Every night for weeks she sat at the kitchen window, often with her friend Margaret Poisson. Ma started after supper and maintained her vigil until the bar closed at 2 a.m. She scrupulously noted every violation—every fight, every use of the alley as a toilet—calling the police to report the noise, the indecent exposures, the fights, and the guys sleeping it off in our yard. She logged the date and time of each call and then went downstairs to talk with the police when they arrived. She also noted the response time and wrote down badge numbers of the officers and what had been done to correct the situation, which was never much. Mostly, the policemen politely promised to talk with the owner and ask him to be more considerate. If they indeed ever did, it didn't help.

One day my mother noticed that the Jefferson Inn's trash had overflowed the concrete receptacle and was piled several feet high outside the bar's back door. "I hate to think what would happen if that ever caught fire," she said.

Jim and I convinced Bill that it was his civic duty to set the trash on fire. The blaze was blistering the paint on the back door of the bar and flames were licking at the roof overhang when a bartender came out and tried to extinguish it by squirting it with a bottle of seltzer water. A neighborhood kid ran to the fire station, and a fireman from Engine 32, around the corner on Hart and Jefferson, came running down the alley carrying a fire extinguisher. While he was trying to knock down the flames, he got too close to the burning trash and his shoelaces caught fire. By the time the fire truck arrived, the fireman with the extinguisher was squirting his burning shoes. The bartender, who had emptied his first seltzer bottle, was back with a fresh one but quickly withdrew into the bar—through the wooden door that was now on fire—after being showered with burning garbage, which had been sent flying by the fire truck's big hoses.

My brothers and I, watching from our upstairs back porch, thought the whole thing was much funnier than any Laurel and Hardy short we had ever seen at the Plaza, the movie theater across from our house. It took the firemen about forty-five minutes to put out the fire and soak down the smoldering trash. The Jefferson Inn was ticketed for creating the situation that caused the fire. My mother duly added this latest incident to her growing list of transgressions, pointing out that the Jefferson Inn's carelessness had endangered the entire neighborhood and that only the quick response of the firemen averted a potential catastrophe.

When she was satisfied that her dossier was complete enough and damning enough, she had her friend Marj Ryan make a typewritten copy for her. Then Ma attached it to a petition that she took to all the neighbors and had them sign it. Even neighbors well out of earshot of the bar's music signed it when my mother convinced them that this kind of creeping blight knew no bounds and had to be stopped before it destroyed the entire neighborhood.

Then she called McClellan Station, the local police precinct, where she managed to speak with the inspector in charge. She explained what she had done, read him the petition, and told him she would get a copy to him the next day. She told him she expected firm and immediate action to remedy the situation. She told the inspector she understood the special nature of the relationship between the police and owners of licensed premises like the Jefferson Inn. She told him that her notes also contained the dates and times of the arrival of marked police cars at the back door of the Jefferson Inn and the exact number of cases of beer and bottles of liquor that had been placed in the trunks of those cars, whose vehicle numbers she had also noted.

She told him that she had not included that information in her petition, because she was not interested in adding to the already substantial burden of the police. But she warned him that if action was not immediate, and if the situation did not improve quickly and dramatically, the information *would* be added to the copy of the petition she planned to send to the mayor, members of the Detroit Common Council, police commissioner, and the editor of the *Detroit Times.*

The police were out the next night, even before the inspector got his copy of the petition. They showed up every night for a week, noting each infraction before finally citing the bar for a long list of violations. The owner ended up in Traffic and Ordinance Court facing a delegation of angry neighbors—all women—led by my mother.

The judge read the complaint and the police report. He said he was troubled by the demonstrated indifference of a business owner to the legitimate concerns of his neighbors. The owner of the Jefferson Inn was fined, ordered to turn down the speakers, and to keep the back door closed. The owner protested that there was no reasonable way to keep people from going out the door into the alley, short of keeping it locked, which was a violation of the fire code. The judge told him to keep an employee stationed at the door to make sure it was not used except in emergencies. Peeing in the alley, the judge said, did not qualify as an emergency. Any violation of the court order could result in serious penalties, including suspension of the bar's license, the judge said.

When my mother left the courtroom with her close friend Margaret Poisson, who had signed the petition even though she lived five or six blocks from the Jefferson Inn, Mrs. Poisson saw my mother smile sweetly and say something to the bar owner as she passed him in the corridor after the hearing. She asked my mother what she said. "I told him I decided not to move," Ma answered.

After the hearing the two women treated themselves to lunch and a hot fudge cream puff sundae at Sanders, the luncheonette and soda fountain on Woodward, before taking the Jefferson streetcar home. It had been a good day.

Things changed dramatically after that. No drunks in the backyard, no more loud music. No Siamese twins or bulls in the alley. No trash fires. We didn't know where Ferdinand was pooping after that, but it wasn't in the Hudson Hotel's parking lot. And whenever some patron managed to slip past the guard at the back door and into the alley, he was quickly grabbed and dragged inside. Before the door was pulled shut, the doorman would look up to see if my mother was watching. She always was.

Truthfully, I missed talking to the entertainers in the alley and rubbing the bull's head. I even missed going into the yard to gingerly nudge sleeping drunks with the toe of my shoe. I always believed the possibility existed that I would, some morning, find a person who had spent the last night of his life in our yard. Going to school and telling the other kids I had found a dead guy in my yard that morning was an adventure I could only imagine.

Mostly, I missed listening to the music, songs that were sad and plaintive reminders of the bucolic lives the young patrons had left behind in the sunny climes they had forsaken for the big-money jobs in the gritty factories of the place they called "De-troit city."

Of course, there were songs about the war, also sad. One was called, "There's a Star-Spangled Banner Waving Somewhere" (1942), most of which I can still sing. It was about a crippled country boy yearning to be able to fight, even die, for his country.

The lines

Though I realize I'm crippled, that is true, sir,
Please don't judge my courage by my twisted leg [always pro-
    nounced "laig" by the vocalist].
Let me show my Uncle Sam what I can do, sir,
Let me help to bring the Axis down a peg

appealed directly to my burgeoning sense of patriotism.

Even with the excitement of the Jefferson Inn successfully repressed, life continued to be interesting at 1532 Lycaste, now that my mother had decided we were not moving. In a decision that reflected the economic exigencies of the time, we rented the nicest bedroom, the one off the front room facing the street, to Tom McKenna, a bachelor from Prince Edward Island, Canada, and a former streetcar motorman. My parents had the bedroom off the dining room, and I shared the room in the back, off the kitchen, with my two brothers.

McKenna, whom we called Wallace, his middle name, worked in the plant at Continental Motors. He also played the harmonica, opening each of his musical sessions with this peppy little toe-tapping rap: "Coffee's in the coffeepot, sugar's in the bowl, Mama's in the kitchen with a little jelly roll."

McKenna had left the Department of Street Railways some years earlier, following an accident on Jefferson Avenue in which the streetcar he was operating struck a girl from Lillibridge Elementary School. Her leg had to be amputated.

He was a hopeless smoker, and his routine every morning was as predictable as the steam whistle that announced the beginning of the workday at the Chrysler plant behind our house. Moments after his feet touched the floor he was lighting his first Chesterfield of the day. After a couple of pulls he started to cough. It was a loud, racking, wet, deep, interminable cough, one we were sure could be heard a block away even with the windows closed. At the breakfast table my father's quiet acknowledgment of this daily event never varied. "McKenna's up," he'd say.

Whenever my mother warned McKenna that he was killing himself with the Chesterfields and needed to see a doctor about his cough, his response was also one we got used to hearing. He would name one of a handful of deceased friends who, he said, would be happy to have his cough.

Chrysler's Jefferson assembly plant, a block or so away from our house, was a block-long expanse of bricks and windows, and the hollow drone that emanated from it was as much a part of the neighborhood as the Fort-Kercheval streetcars that rattled noisily down Lycaste and past our front door day and night. The factory was topped with a huge, lighted "Chrysler DeSoto" sign that around 1945 became "Chrysler Fluid Drive" when the company felt confident enough about its new transmission system to brag about it in lights. The sign dominated the neighborhood and brightened our back bedroom every night, washing the painted walls in light and then returning the room to darkness every fifteen seconds or so. The cycle was precisely timed, on hot summer nights when sleep failed, by a kid who imagined he had the power to make the great sign go off and on merely by snapping his fingers.

But outweighing 1532 Lycaste's unsuitable location near heavy manufacturing was its location just across the street from the Plaza Theatre. If a single element—outside of church and school—dominated our lives, it was the movie theater. Every Saturday and Sunday we indulged our wildest fantasies, sitting through endless screenings of westerns, war movies, high-seas swashbucklers, melodramas, jungle adventures, and happy musicals. On any given weekend we could be found sharing the Round Table with King Arthur, on the trail with Hopalong Cassidy or Johnny Mack Brown, breaking up over the Three Stooges, swinging through the hot African jungle with Tarzan, or talking tough with the Dead End Kids on some dusty street in Hell's Kitchen.

To be sure, we watched movies with what passed for steamy love scenes, but for kids in their early teens they held little appeal, at least at that point in our lives. We thought people kissing each other was a certified waste of time, especially when they could just as easily have been shooting at each other or throwing cream pies.

But movies' potential to suck impressionable children into the corrupt morass of sins of the flesh was not lost on my mother. Inspired by an enthusiastic clergy, she stood resolutely between her children and the evils of Hollywood, a mother determined to protect us from anything that might jeopardize our salvation.

So, once a year, we stood up in church, raised our right hands, and took the pledge of the Catholic Legion of Decency, vowing to live pure lives and to keep the taint of sin from finding its way into our souls through indecent films, which my father called *fillums*. Ma watched us carefully as we pledged, making sure we spoke the words clearly and were not just mumbling them as a hedge against any intended future violation of the precepts.

As a family we pledged solemnly to "condemn all indecent and immoral motion pictures, and those which glorify crime or criminals." I was never sure what my personal pledge to "do all that I can to strengthen public opinion against the production of indecent and immoral films, and to unite with all who protest against them" actually involved. Nonetheless, I acknowledged before God, Mae Shine, and those sitting closest to us in St. Rose Church "my obligation to form a right conscience about pictures that are dangerous to my moral life . . . to remain away from them . . . and to stay away altogether from places of amusement which show them as a matter of policy," which, as far as I could tell, probably did not include the Plaza.

Each week, long before Hollywood instituted a ratings system, the Michigan Catholic newspaper published a list of movies rated by category and provided by the Legion of Decency. The ratings were broken down into four main groups, Class A, Section I ("Everybody May See These"); Class A, Section II ("Adults May Enjoy These"); Class B ("Children Stay Away! Adults Be Very Careful!"), and Class C, Condemned ("Hold Your Nose While Passing By!").

When Jimmy Thomas, our downstairs neighbor, took all the neighborhood kids to the East End Theatre as part of his 1941 birthday celebration, my brothers and I were not allowed to go. The movie they went to see, *Dr. Jekyll and Mr. Hyde,* was not on the approved list.

Each week Ma taped the list to the kitchen wall, and although we were allowed to see only the A-I movies, we could read the complete list, if only as an empty exercise to see what we were missing. What we were missing were a lot of really good war movies listed as A-IIs, movies like *Remember Pearl Harbor* (1942), *A Yank in Libya* (1942), *Eagle Squadron* (1942), *Parachute Nurse* (1942), and *I Escaped from the Gestapo* (1943). If Ma had any concerns that her children were being denied access to contemporary history, she was not concerned enough to loosen the rules.

We read the list of condemned movies, not because we thought one of them might slip unnoticed into the Plaza or the East End, but because we were overcome by fantasies, not yet fully formed, of sitting alone in the dark, sweaty and dry-mouthed, watching movies with titles like *Souls in Pawn* (1940), *Fools of Desire* (1941), and *Delinquent Daughters* (1944).

My mother read the C list as carefully as she read the other three, if only to reassure herself that none of these licentious offerings had, through some typographical accident, moved from C to A-I. I'm sure she thought it was the least she could do as a mother eager to protect the souls of her children. I'm also sure that she cross-checked *Romance on the Range* (a 1942 Roy Rogers film) against the C's before she allowed us to see it.

When my mother spotted in her oldest son what appeared to be the beginnings of a natural hormone-driven curiosity about girls, she regarded it as a frightening precursor to the wild trumpeting of the flesh that would most certainly follow.

To me it was fairly simple. I was starting to like girls in a way that was different from how I had liked them before. I liked Betty Brady and Shirley Ann Rowles, who lived on our street and were playmates, but I *liked* Patricia Ames, who was in my class at St. Rose School. By the time I was in high school, my mother was taking a new interest in every aspect of my existence outside the home. She wanted to know where I was going, with whom, what we would be doing, where we were meeting, and what time I was coming home. She was a relentless interrogator, but I was, for my age, an effective dissembler. I lied with an alarming facility and an impressive quickness.

When she suspected that I was going to be spending my time in the company of girls, she talked about the near occasion of sin and the unpleasant and everlasting consequences of just one small lapse: an eternity of fiery torment for a moment of illicit pleasure. We were reminded in school that the real pain of hell was not in the endless fires that would burn our bodies without consuming them but in the realization that we were condemned to spend eternity without ever seeing the face of God. At the time, I was, frankly, more worried about the fire than about not seeing God's face.

We were also made to understand fully that eternity was a very long time. To help us comprehend just how long, the nuns asked us to imagine a solid steel ball, five hundred times larger than Earth, and that every thousand years a sparrow flew past and brushed the ball with its wing. When the ball was worn away to nothing, we were told, eternity would just be beginning. It was a sobering concept.

And on the off chance that we were not sufficiently aware of the fate that awaited sinners, our fear of everlasting damnation was reinforced two or three times a year during missions conducted by visiting Redemptorist or Passionist priests whose universal theme seemed to be the inevitability of postmortem suffering.

I clearly remember the evening one of them described, in frightening detail, the everlasting fires of hell and the horrible agony of the damned. Among the shrieks of the lost souls, he said, a tiny voice could be heard begging for a single drop of water. Lips cracked and bleeding, tongue black and swollen, the doomed creature cried out in that sulfurous wasteland, "Water! For the love of God, one drop of water!" The priest repeated the phrase over and over, his rasping voice growing weaker until the last faint gasp of "Water!" echoed through the silent church as he swept out of the pulpit and quickly disappeared into the sacristy. I ran all the way home that night and drank three or four glasses of water, then went to bed and dreamed about hell.

When I ultimately confronted the occasion of sin on my own terms, I found it less disagreeable than I had been led to expect. One summer night in 1944 I got my first serious kiss, warm, moist, and prolonged, from Rosemary Kane on the front porch of her house on Montclair. I went a bit light-headed, lost my balance, and very nearly tumbled over the wooden railing into the Kanes' spirea bush. I was fourteen and knew at that moment my life had taken a wonderful new turn. Thoughts of the steel ball began to fade.

My mother must have suspected that things were changing. She started waiting up for me every night, grilling me on my activities of that evening. But I always had my story ready, keeping it simple and straightforward so she would have difficulty picking it apart. I knew enough not to comb my hair as I walked up Lycaste because I knew she would be watching from behind the curtains in our front room and would know immediately that any boy combing his hair while coming into his house at night had had it tousled by unauthorized hands during unauthorized activity.

One summer evening I indulged in a sustained romantic interlude with a girl from Southeastern High School along the banks of the Detroit River. I was too busy kissing her to brush away the horde of mosquitoes that had landed on my back, drilled through my flimsy white cotton T-shirt, and feasted without interruption on my suddenly warmer-than-usual blood.

When my mother saw the angry red eruptions peppered across my back the next morning she said, "Jesus, Mary, and Joseph! What happened to your back?"

"Mosquito bites," I replied matter-of-factly, casually reading the Wheaties box and unwilling to give her more information than that to work with. When she pushed some more, I told her I was bitten while I was down near the canals with some of the guys from school, trying to make it sound like thirty or forty mosquito bites on your back was simply the price you paid for living as close as we did to standing water.

Her failure to pursue the matter surprised me because she almost never ended the questioning until she was satisfied with the quality of the answers, which she almost never was. As an investigator she was without peer. She could, for example, spot a residual fleck of lipstick at twenty paces in dim light.

"What's that on your mouth?" she would ask, squinting in the dark, knowing that if my hand shot up reflexively to wipe my mouth, it was a sure sign of guilt.

"Red pop," I would answer, hands at my side.

On nights when I came home suffering temporary paralysis of the lips caused by the kind of intense and long-term necking we called "smash mouth," I prayed she would not stop in the middle of the interrogation and ask: "Why are you talking like that?"

In this hormonally confused period of my life I also had to contend with a continuing plague of what were referred to in general

terms as "impure thoughts." Even as I was having my first ones—
which I think was quite early—I knew they were not morally defen-
sible.

My grade-school book, *A Catechism Primer of Christian Doctrine,* which offers a primer in sin, was one of the treasures my
mother consigned to the green box. She had re-covered it with
brown paper cut from a grocery bag and carefully stitched it in
place with black thread. It is a fifty-page booklet, a slender out-
line of Catholic tenets written to make sure God's children were
moving in the proper spiritual direction early in life. It presents the
basic rules of the church in question-and-answer format. On page
sixteen, which someone in another time (my mother?) had marked
with a pencil, is Lesson VII, titled simply: "SIN."

> Question Number 4: "Is it a sin to think bad thoughts?"
> Answer: **"It is a sin to think bad thoughts."**

Even though I knew it had apparently been a sin to think bad
thoughts at least since 1910 when the booklet was published, I was,
it seemed, powerless to do anything about them. They seemed to take
possession of my brain, unbidden, crowding out everything else. My
mind was constantly besieged by them. They flashed through my
consciousness like runaway motion pictures on a continuous loop.
During confession every Friday afternoon I ducked into the dark
box to relieve myself of this sinful burden. When the disembodied
voice on the other side of the wooden grille asked ominously, "How
many times?" I was always too embarrassed to even approximate
the real number. I could imagine the stunned priest stumbling back
to the rectory in a daze, asking himself how a kid my age could possibly have that many impure thoughts in one week unless it was the
only thing he did. I sometimes think it *was* the only thing I did.

So each week I provided a high double-digit number, far short
of my estimated total but one I hoped the priest would accept as
reasonable and a figure that might, in God's eyes, fall under the
umbrella of some kind of general sacramental amnesty known as
"close enough."

I remember hearing Max Mireault, a neighbor who was French Canadian, tell my father once that although he could speak English, he thought in French. In the confessional, for example, he said he had to recall his sins in French, translate them in his head, and recite the English version to the priest. I recall wondering if this provided Mr. Mireault with any kind of penitential benefit denied to monolinguals. I could envision entire categories of spiritual and moral transgressions being softened considerably by something that could be defended as "lost in translation."

But the closest I ever got to a language advantage was at St. Bonaventure, the Capuchin monastery on Mt. Elliott. It was the place my classmates and I went to confess sins too sensitive to be trusted to the local clergy. Even though we were assured in our religion classes that in the confessional we were protected by some kind of sacramental anonymity, we didn't buy it. One Saturday afternoon, after I had finished confessing my sins, including my usual low-ball estimate of impure thoughts, Father Matt Blake, calling me by name, gave me fifteen cents and asked me to go to the St. Rose Sweet Shop across from church, get him a pack of cigarettes, and bring them to the side door of the church. So much for the oft-repeated assurance by the nuns that "what you say in confession is strictly between you and God."

So, even though it was about forty blocks from our neighborhood, the monastery was our fallback penitential venue. One week we came across a priest there whose mastery of English was severely limited, enabling us, in one afternoon, to rid ourselves of an impressive accumulation of sins we did not feel comfortable discussing within the St. Rose parish boundaries. This, of course, included my own backlog of impure thoughts.

As painful and frightening as the confessional experience could be, I still remember the wonderful feeling of lightness as I left the confessional at St. Rose, my soul cleansed of the stain of sin, and headed to the altar rail to say my penance of ten Our Fathers and ten Hail Marys, my Buster Brown oxfords barely touching the floor. Then I would spot Helen McGuire or Geraldine Colombo waiting her turn to go into the confessional, and before I could even ponder the consequences, the impure thoughts meter would begin running again.

I also spent a lot of time trying to take advantage of the moral ambiguity I saw in this whole impure thoughts thing. If those images came to me uninvited and without my encouragement, wasn't it reasonable to believe that no serious spiritual damage would result? It wasn't a particularly strong theological principle but, absent anything better, I embraced it.

At home, meanwhile, the pressure remained constant, especially now that I was a junior in high school, and especially, it seemed, during May, the month of the Blessed Virgin, the patroness of purity. My mother had special devotion to Mary, for whom she had been named, and prayed to her regularly and devoutly for all her special intentions. A nun manqué, we would have suspected, if we had known what that meant.

One of the hymns we sang in May was "Mother Dear, O Pray for Me." One of the verses began:

Mother dear, O pray for me
Should pleasure's siren lay
E'er tempt thy child to wander far
From virtue's path away.

I dared not look at my mother during the "pleasure's siren" part, but I could feel her eyes burning into me, especially during the part of the refrain that asked the Virgin to "never cease thy care, till in heaven eternally thy love and bliss I share."

What my mother didn't know was that I was already sharing love and bliss, at a more temporal level, with an adorable ninth-grader, Phyllis Knowles, who was new to St. Rose and with whom I was soon hopelessly smitten.

During the next weeks and months I leaked a few harmless details about the relationship to my mother, who saw nothing harmless in it at all. She turned up the heat. She suspected, correctly, that I was spending a lot of time with this girl. Ma's daily refrain became, "Why don't you give that poor girl a rest?" At that stage of my infatuation resting was not part of the plan.

The next year I got a serious case of food poisoning, and one evening, just after I had been released from the hospital, a group of school friends came to see me. I was still confined to bed so they all crowded into my small bedroom in the flat on Lycaste. McKenna had moved to an upstairs flat in Grosse Pointe Park, and I had been promoted to the front bedroom, away from the alternating light-then-dark monotony of the Chrysler sign. The adorable ninth-grader—now an adorable tenth-grader—sat on the edge of my bed holding my hand that evening.

When my mother came into the room and saw her, she shot me one of her withering looks that said silently but clearly, "Get that girl off your bed this minute!" I spent the rest of the evening avoiding eye contact with my mother and holding tight to the hand of the girl on my bed. I'm sure my mother was relieved six years later when I married the girl, taking, Mae Shine believed, the only honorable path open to me after we had shared that level of intimacy.

I lived most of my life believing that none of this was my mother's fault, that she was, indeed, an innocent country girl and had been raised in this puritanical Catholic ethic by an overly strict father, who believed, as she did now, that keeping company put the soul at risk and that what seemed like innocent flirtations were the first sweet steps on the road to damnation.

Then I got the letter from Tommy Doyle.

Tommy was born and raised in Carrick-on-Shannon and wrote me from Edgware, Middlesex, England, where he was living. Someone had sent him a copy of a St. Patrick's Day story I had written in 1982 for the *Detroit Free Press*'s *Sunday Magazine* about growing up Irish. The story carried a picture I had taken on my visit to Carrick in 1954 of his mother, Hannah Doyle, standing with my grandmother, Bridget Conlon, at the front gate of the Conlon house. The world being a small place and Carrick even smaller, Tommy turned out to be the nephew of Katie Dolan, the midwife who had delivered my mother.

He wrote that he enjoyed the story and thought the picture of his mother was wonderful. Then he talked about Mae Conlon, whom he called "that young, very beautiful, kind and gentle lady."

"When your mother left Carrick," he wrote, "I saw grown men and boys cry. The boys went out to the station and hid behind the hedge. . . . When the train pulled out, they bawled their eyes out. All have been called home now. Matt Jack, Jim Feely, John Dolan, Harry McGowan, John Gavin, Johnnie Gill, Paddy Hart, J. P. Murry, old John Lavin, the blacksmith. They were all in love with your mother. If she smiled at them it made their day. God rest their souls."

There were nine names. Not bad, I thought, for an eighteen-year-old in a small Irish town with James Conlon for a father.

Tommy wrote about how much he liked the Conlons and told me that when they moved from the laborer's cottage on the Leitrim Road in 1928, he dug up the rose tree near their front door and transplanted it to the new house on Kingston Terrace. It had still been there when I visited twenty-six years later. But he spoke only obliquely in the letter about his own affection for Mae Conlon. He did tell me that shortly after she left for America, he went off and joined the French Foreign Legion. He didn't say why.

When I showed my mother the letter, she said Tommy had wildly overstated the extent of those friendships, and she allowed that maybe his memory was suffering the predictable effects of too many days in the Algerian sun without his kepi. Then, as she re-read Tommy's two pages of block printing, she conceded, between smiles and a few tears, that perhaps there was a small measure of truth in what he wrote, adding quickly that she shouldn't be held responsible for how some of the young men in Carrick might have felt about her. Besides, she said, there certainly was no encouragement from her in any of this.

She also said that what Tommy Doyle—and apparently the nine

others—did not know was that she was engaged, secretly, to a Carrick boy when she left. We have no way of knowing for sure, but Seamus and her sisters are convinced that it was Willie McNutt, the forbidden Protestant. The plan, her sisters told my brothers and me when we visited them in England in 2004, was for Willie to join her after she had been in America for a time so they could get married without having to concern themselves with family disapproval on either side.

I remember Ma telling us once that when she boarded the ship in Cobh, she took off the ring and put it in her pocket, perhaps seeing it as an impediment to making new friends in the new world. Willie McNutt never came to America. It is probably logical to believe that he might not have been able to afford passage or that distance had become an impossible barrier even for young love to overcome. Or both. If he ever wrote her, none of his letters survived to be tucked away in the green box.

Whatever his reasons, Willie McNutt stayed in Carrick-on-Shannon. On June 29, 1929, Mae Conlon married Patrick J. Shine in St. Charles Church on Detroit's East Side. Willie McNutt, who never married, drowned with two others on May 19, 1933, when their racing shell capsized on the Shannon during a practice run for the town's annual regatta.

On May 27, 1933, the *Leitrim Observer* carried the story of the tragedy on its front page:

APPALLING DROWNING DISASTER
ON THE SHANNON

A drowning tragedy of a magnitude which horrified the public occurred on the Shannon near Carrick-on-Shannon on Friday evening, resulting in the loss of three valuable lives, and plunging their families into mourning, which will last until this generation passes.

The story goes on to describe the three young men as "the finest types of manhood in the town and district, of a popularity which was undeniable, and all around ardent sportsmen." The *Observer* listed the dead as P. Conneely, 29, a policeman; Patrick Rooney, 26, a motor mechanic; and William McNutt, 29, a building contractor.

My youngest brother was born three years later. My mother named him William.

Mae Conlon Shine's rigid position on the perils of company keeping softened considerably after her three sons were safely married. That she failed to apply the same kind of severe moral judgments to succeeding generations became clear one day in 1979.

When Jim, our oldest son, graduated from college, he bought a house on the street where my mother lived. At some point he decided to share living quarters with his girlfriend, Deanna Groehn (later to become Deanna "Dede" Shine), a decision not given wide circulation among the family.

My mother, of course, knew right away. She was a one-woman Neighborhood Watch, and nothing of note took place in her environment that she did not know about. She kept it to herself. We learned of Jim's house-sharing arrangement and also of my mother's prior knowledge of it at about the same time. When I asked my mother how long she had known about it, she told me she had Jim—more precisely, James Conlon Shine—and his girlfriend to her house for dinner the week Dede moved in.

I asked her why she hadn't mentioned it to me. Because it was none of my business, she told me. I told her I was shocked by her change of heart and speculated that she might not have been as dismissive if it had been me in the same situation.

"Oh, for God's sake," she said in her most exasperated tone, "get with it. It's the seventies."

Private James Conlon in the uniform of the Connaught Rangers, 1903.

The girls of the Marist Convent School in Carrick-on-Shannon.
Mary Ellen Conlon is fifth from left in top row.

The bridal party, June 29, 1929. *Standing:* Michael Shine and Annie Riley; *seated:* the bride and groom, Patrick Joseph Shine and Mary Ellen Conlon Shine.

Last day at sea on the SS *Republic,* United States Lines, 1927.
Mary Ellen Conlon is at the center left of the group, near the rail,
with short hair and a pointed collar over her sweater.

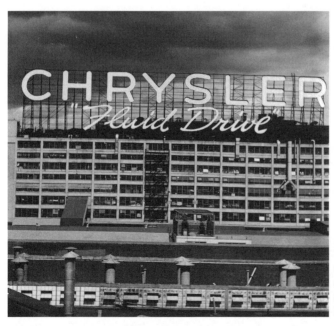

The lighted sign atop
the Chrysler Jeffer-
son plant behind the
Shine house, 1532
Lycaste, ca. 1945.

Mae and her sons at a picnic in
Chandler Park, 1940; *from left:*
Jim, Bill, and Neal.

The Guinness depot from the Shannon Bridge, 2004.

Bridge Street, Carrick-on-Shannon, 2004.

The Bradshaw house in St. George's Terrace, 2004.
Mary Ellen Conlon worked here from 1923 to 1927.

Jim and Bill on the front steps of the Shine house at 1532 Lycaste, 1948.

Mae and Neal in Ireland, 1984.

Bridget Conlon, Neal's grandmother, in the front garden at 4 Kingston Terrace, Carrick-on-Shannon, 1954, with Tommy Doyle's rose tree behind her.

Mae and Neal in the backyard of the Shine house at 1532 Lycaste, June 13, 1948, the day he graduated from St. Rose High School.

Mae holding Jim with Neal at her feet, 1932.

Pat Shine with sons Jim (*left*) and Neal on a Sunday walk, 1937.

Life with Mae

Looking back, my brothers and I realized that life with Mae Shine was anything but routine, and over the years we came to suspect that she might not have been what God had in mind when he invented mothers.

She was, as were most mothers in the neighborhood, the fierce defender of the clan. She took our part in squabbles with neighborhood kids or their parents and then, more often than not, walloped us when she got us home for creating the situation in the first place. She said she was not interested in continually embarrassing herself by standing up for us to people she didn't know over disputes that were probably our fault all along.

When I was six or seven, a new girl on our block, Lois Poisson, smacked me on the head with a coal shovel for some perceived annoyance. My mother promptly marched me, and the dusty lump on my head, to the Poisson house two doors away to confront Mrs. Poisson and her felonious daughter.

My mother explained quietly to Mrs. Poisson that she considered assault with a coal shovel an extreme way to settle childhood disagreements. Mrs. Poisson agreed and made her daughter, who was better known as "Peachy," apologize. Then Mrs. Poisson made tea for my mother, and the two of them—by now it was "Mae" and "Margaret"—spent the rest of the afternoon talking and laughing together while I sat uncomfortably next to my mother as Peachy glared at me from across the room. Before we left, my mother decided that my culpability in the incident was probably greater than she had first believed and made me, in turn, apologize to Peachy.

I apologized, still not quite able to reconcile the girl's sweet nickname with the malevolent look on her face when she hit me with the shovel. Nor did I fully understand why I, clearly the aggrieved party, was now being required to say I was sorry for getting hit on the head. On the way home my mother berated me for antagonizing such a lovely little girl and for aggravating Peachy to the point where she found it necessary to brain me with a heavy shovel. By the time we got home, I found myself touching the knot on my head to reassure myself that it had all really happened the way I remembered.

The long-term result of the coal shovel incident was a friendship between the Shines and the Poissons that would last forty-five years. Peachy and I became close pals, the coal shovel affair always the thing that seemed to bond us. I went to her wedding and the christening of her children and then to her funeral a few years ago. Her children and grandchildren asked me to tell them again about the day of the coal shovel.

As children we lived what seemed to us to be a fairly normal existence. We had no other mother in the house against whom we could measure maternal performance so we had to assume that all mothers were like ours. We probably believed that all mothers collected the dog poop deposited on their front lawn, put it in a paper bag, and then, under cover of night, took it to the house where the owner of the offending dog lived and dumped it on the porch.

I remember my mother coming into the house, out of breath from running home after one of her dog poop missions, giggling at the prospect of the offending dog's owner exiting his front door on his way to work the next morning and stepping in the mess she had left on his doormat.

"I'd love to see the look on that gobshite's face tomorrow when he steps in it," she would say, followed by another burst of laughter.

Next to "Jesus, Mary, and Joseph!" an invocation she used frequently to express frustration, surprise, anger, dismay, or a sense of general unhappiness at what was going on around her, *gobshite* was as close as she ever came to swearing when we were young, although we would hear an occasional *hell* or *damn.*

As she grew older and worried less about convention, her language became a bit more earthy, especially when she felt the need to express herself in the shortest and most direct way possible. It was as if she felt that the older she got, the less time she had for convoluted and wordy assaults to convey her annoyance with a person or a situation when a one- or two-word expletive would be a shorter and more effective way to get the same message across. She was interested in conveying the maximum amount of transgressive power with a minimum of effort. Add to all this the predictable impact of hearing language like that coming from a sweet, gray-haired old lady, and you might understand why it was a combination that appealed to her.

One morning when she was in her mid-seventies, she was shopping in the neighborhood Kroger store when a well-dressed man in a business suit banged his shopping cart noisily into hers as he tried to make his way past her. The man complained loudly about its being impossible to shop anymore without being surrounded by indecisive old women reading every label on every package and blocking the aisles in the process.

She smiled at him graciously, moved her cart out of the way, and then suggested sweetly what he could go and do to himself. The man stood in stunned silence for several seconds before he fled the store, leaving his cart full of groceries in the aisle. Telling my wife and me about it later that week, Ma said, without the slightest hint of remorse, "God forgive me, I don't know what got into me. It was out of me before I could stop myself." Then she began to laugh as she said, with undisguised glee, "You should have seen the look on him." She also told us, based on how he was dressed, that she thought he might have been a lawyer, a circumstance she probably thought reduced her offense in the eyes of God to no more than a venial sin.

She sometimes used the word *hoor*, a throwback to her Irishness. The word has only a root relationship to its loosely homophonic sister. Its meaning can be, but is not always, pejorative. If an Irish farmer tells his neighbor that he got an exceptionally good price for a heifer on fair day, the neighbor might well exclaim, "Ah, ye hoor, ye!" shaking the farmer's hand in admiration.

Phil O'Dwyer, a friend who was born and raised in Tipperary, told me once about a man in his hometown who was known to stop of a Saturday for a pint at the pub across from church. One Saturday the man left the pub and slipped into the last pew as Mass was being said. He quickly dozed off.

Near the end of Mass the priest was leading the parishioners in the renewal of their baptismal vows. When the pastor boomed, "Do you reject Satan and all his works and all his empty promises?" the startled man opened his eyes and answered loudly, "Ah, we do, the hoor!"

My mother sometimes used the phrase "hoor's get" (illegitimate offspring of a woman of loose virtue) to describe those people she considered to be irretrievably unpleasant. That she used it as sparingly as she did impressed on us the seriousness of the designation.

At some point while I was in high school, we were instructed to write "JMJ" (Jesus, Mary, and Joseph) at the top of our papers as a way of inviting the Holy Family to bless and inspire our work. In my case it was an invitation that mostly went unacknowledged. I was always convinced that if I had shown those papers, all properly headed "JMJ," to my mother, she would have taken one look at the letter grade the nun had written on the paper—too often a U (unsatisfactory) or a D, only marginally better than a U—and loudly invited the unabbreviated Jesus, Mary, and Joseph to join in her disappointment at my scholarship deficit.

While her habit of invoking the intercession of the Holy Family often ran close to the narrow line that separates prayer from expletive, there was never the same confusion about *gobshite*. It was her favorite one-word description of people she actively disliked, and it was clear to us from the way she said it that it was not a nice word.

It's an Irish expression that does not translate readily to English. One dictionary of slang terms lists thirteen definitions of *gobshite*, none reaching a level my mother would have considered adequate.

We were not allowed to use *gobshite* in front of her, but at some point as young kids we learned what apparently was a particularly vile Italian swear word from a neighbor kid, and we took to using it freely around the house. Because romance languages were clearly not part of the curriculum at her convent school in Carrick, Ma had no idea what it meant, nor did we. When we continued to use it freely as a noun, an adverb, an adjective, or an exclamation, laughing wildly as we did, her natural curiosity was aroused. One day she repeated the word for Mrs. Ferreri, our Italian-born neighbor, and asked her if she knew what it meant. Instead of answering, Mrs. Ferreri put her hand to her mouth in horror, ran back into her house, and slammed the door.

My mother came home, lined us up, gave each of us a wallop, and told us it was just a sample of what we would get if we ever used the word again. We were puzzled at getting smacked for using a word that she didn't even understand but were smart enough not to use it again in front of her. When my brothers and I are together, we occasionally slip the word into the conversation. It still makes us laugh.

Whenever I am asked to describe the cultural advantage of growing up in an ethnically diverse neighborhood, my answer is that I can swear in eight languages.

At some point late in life my mother embraced the practice of extending the middle finger as an indication of her displeasure, "flipping the bird," as it is sometimes called. This happened most often while she was riding with one of us in the car. If someone committed what she considered an egregious breach of road courtesy or blew a horn at us, she looked at the offending driver until she caught his eye and, smiling sweetly, gave him the finger. At the same time she would offer a thought: "Up yours with a wire brush."

By the time she was in her mid-seventies her hands were so crippled with arthritis that it was difficult for her to straighten her finger enough for an effective gesture. But she was not deterred. Those at whom it was directed still got the message. Bill still insists the gnarled finger and swollen knuckles added special impact.

But Ma doing strange or quirky things in her later years was not unusual. We, as her kids, had witnessed that type of behavior all our lives. For instance, we did not find it odd on the Monday she got up at 3 a.m. to do her wash. She wanted to get it hung out before dawn just once to outdo Mrs. Fries. She was our next-door neighbor on Beniteau and always had her wash on the line before 8 a.m. on Monday and always gloated insufferably—"A little late this morning are we, Mrs. Shine?"—when Ma came out to hang her wash three hours later.

We also had to assume that kitchen-sink baptism was an accepted extension of the sacrament sanctioned by the Vatican to help bring church ritual into the home.

My mother always knew which relatives or friends had been derelict, by her standards, in getting a child baptized as soon after its birth as possible. Her standards meant no longer than a week, two at the most.

So whenever a young mother showed up at our house with an unbaptized baby that was more than a month old, my mother would pick up the child, fuss over it for a few minutes, and then drift almost imperceptibly toward the kitchen. When we heard the water running in the sink, my brothers and I would smile slyly at each other because we knew that the rite of conditional baptism was being conferred on yet another pagan baby. She would come back into the room, dabbing at wet hair with a dish towel and saying something about the heat—even in winter—and how the poor thing seemed to be sweating.

But there was always a smile on her face. She had just saved another child from the emptiness of limbo, that intermediate place between heaven and hell to which helpless infants were consigned if they died before their shiftless, backsliding parents had bothered to have them baptized.

When my mother did something that many would consider a breach of good conduct, there was no sense getting upset or objecting. If she thought it needed to be done, she did it, and that was good enough for her. Case closed. So that's why I never mustered even a mild protest when she told me one day in January 1953 that she had invited Harold Lemmer, the plumber who was fixing the pipes in our bathroom, to be the soloist at my wedding later that month. She had heard him singing while he worked on her shower, thought he had a nice voice, and asked him if he'd like to sing at her son's wedding.

He quickly accepted her offer and said he would sing "Panis Angelicus" and "Ave Maria" during the wedding Mass at St. Margaret Mary Church. I remember exchanging a nervous glance with my bride as the first notes of "Panis Angelicus" drifted from the organ in the choir loft behind us. But Harold Lemmer had an exceptionally nice voice, and we all suspected that Mae had future plumbing bills discounted nicely for providing this impressive change of venue for a man who did much of his singing in other people's bathrooms.

Nor were we the least bit horrified when she returned from a visit to Ireland and mentioned, in passing, that she had offered to be an accomplice to homicide. One of her closest childhood friends, who still lived in Carrick, told my mother in pathetic detail about the terrible turn her life had taken since her marriage. They were walking out the Priest Lane in Carrick while her friend spoke of how her husband was physically abusing her.

"Mae," she lamented tearfully, "I don't know what I'm going to do."

"I tell you what I'd do," my mother answered. "I'd kill him."

"Oh, Jesus, Mary, and Joseph, Mae!" her friend said, horrified, no longer crying. "Don't say things like that."

"I'm serious," my mother said. "I'd never let a man lay a hand on me, and neither should you."

My mother went on to suggest that the woman put rat poison in her husband's tea, the sooner the better. She even offered to go to the hardware store and buy the poison for her and help her determine what might be a fatal dose.

As far as we know, the plot ended there, but my mother always insisted that none of it was a joke. If you're going to kill someone, she reasoned, what better place to do it than some small town in Ireland?

This is how she envisioned her friend could get away with murder: After the husband fell face down on the table, the wife would dump what was left of the toxic tea in the garden, rinse the cup, and then ring up the police barracks. She'd tell the sergeant that her husband, who had been complaining of chest pains for several days, had had a heart attack and died at the kitchen table. Then she'd send a neighbor kid off to the doctor's house to get the death certificate signed. No autopsy, no test for toxins, no investigation. A nice wake, an equally nice funeral. One bad husband permanently out of the way.

This relaxed approach to premature death in rural Ireland seemed to be reinforced by Seamus's recollections: "If you ever needed a death certificate, you'd go to this one old doctor who always carried a pad [of death certificates] with him. You could always find him in the pub, and you'd come in and say, 'Paddy McGinty's died above in Lisnagot,' and he'd say, 'Gimme two shillings and I'll write out a death certificate for you.'" The official medical determination was always "natural causes" with no need to even see the deceased, Seamus said.

Brother Bill added his own classic ending to the crime that never happened. "After the funeral Ma would have marched back to the hardware store with what was left of the poison, asking for at least a partial refund because she had used only a couple of teaspoons. Then she'd give the money to the widow to help offset the cost of the wake." We agreed that it was a believable final act to the drama.

Mae Shine seemed to have the same kind of quirky relationship with death and dying as most of our Irish friends and relatives. Stories of wakes and funerals enjoyed a wide popularity in our house, as did an entire genre of funny stories about them. My father loved telling about the Kerry farmer who went on a tour to the Soviet Union and visited Lenin's Tomb in Moscow. After viewing the Communist leader's remains, the farmer walked solemnly up to the soldier standing guard outside the tomb, shook his hand, and said, "Sorry for your trouble."

It's probably the reason my mother seemed to spend an inordinate amount of time in funeral homes. She considered it an inexcusable breach of etiquette not to call at the funeral home to express regrets at the passing of a friend or neighbor, even if the friendship was tenuous and the dead person someone she'd hardly spoken to.

Whenever I accompanied her to a funeral home, especially a large one like Verheyden's, she insisted on looking into all the viewing rooms just in case she had even a fleeting acquaintance with the deceased or knew any of the mourners who happened to be there at the time. If it turned out that she knew neither the deceased nor any of the family, she passed herself off to the next of kin as "a neighbor," falling back on Christ's broadest definition of the category. She extended condolences, knelt at the casket and offered a prayer, signed the book, and took a prayer card, explaining to me on the way out, "Well, whoever she was, she can certainly use an extra prayer."

My suspicion is that, as often as not, she went to the funeral home just to get a look at the casket. Although it might not be fair to call it a serious preoccupation of hers, she was definitely interested in the style of the conveyance in which her friends and neighbors were being delivered to their eternal rest.

Even more fascinating, however, was the fine line she drew between what she considered shameless corner cutting in one instance and showy extravagance in another. Whenever a neighbor called to tell her, "Mae, get up to Doherty's this minute, and get a look at the casket poor Margaret Carmody's laid out in," she would put all else aside, comb her hair, grab her hat and purse, and hurry off to the funeral home.

What followed was a few weeks' worth of casket dialogues

with her lady friends. On the one hand she would tsk-tsk at Peter Carmody's shameless penny pinching in "poor Margaret's" case, then express shock at the disgraceful way in which another family had lavished a major portion of the insurance money on an ostentatious casket.

The ladies would lament the spending of "that kind of money" on something that's going to end up in the ground when it would have done more good to send some of it to the Jesuits or the Maryknoll Fathers, who would say Masses around the clock for the deceased. The suggestions about how the money might have been better spent often went something like this: "She would've gotten more use from a nice new stove than she'll ever get from a fancy casket she never even got to see." This would, in turn, prompt further discussion of the deceased's old stove and how she—God have mercy on her—ever managed to cook a decent meal on such a relic.

My mother's willingness to deal face-to-face with death did not stop her from being wildly superstitious and a quiet but devoted believer in things supernatural. We were still in grade school when we got up one Monday morning and found her sleeping, fully dressed, on the couch where she had spent the night. She told us she had been listening to a radio show called *The Hermit's Cave,* which was broadcast late on Sunday nights. It was always an effectively frightening half hour that opened with the hermit, in a sinister croak, ordering the listeners to "Turn out your lights, turn them out!" My mother listened in the dark and found that night's story so terrifying that when it ended at midnight, she was too frightened to get off the couch to turn the lights back on.

She was especially wary of a house near us on Beniteau that was empty when we moved to that street and still empty when we left nearly eight years later. It was gray and weather-beaten, and its front yard was overgrown with tall weeds. Hedges, left to grow wild, crowded the sidewalk. Nobody ever went near it, not even the nosy neighborhood kids who had somehow decided that the owner of the house had been murdered there and was buried beneath the concrete floor of the basement. Neighborhood legend was that if you peeked through one of the grimy basement windows, you could see the spot in the floor where a rectangle of newer cement had been poured. None of us ever looked. My mother told us years later that whenever she approached the house after dark, she moved into the middle of the street and ran as fast as she could until she was safely past it.

Her superstitions were endless, and she took pains not to violate any of them. She believed it was bad luck to look at a new moon through glass, to take a shaker of salt directly from the hand of another, to pass someone on a staircase who was going the opposite way, or to leave a house by a door other than the one through which you had entered. A hat left on a bed meant a row, so did new shoes put on a table, and dropped cutlery meant company was coming. Stir with a knife, stir up strife. A robin sitting on a fence was a harbinger of death, and if someone's picture fell from the wall for no apparent reason, that person would be the next to die. If a bird flew into a house, someone in the family was going to die soon. An expectant woman seeing magpies singly or in a group of as many as four could tell the gender or temperament of her baby: "One for a girl, two for a boy, three for sorrow, four for joy." If you discover during the day that you donned an article of clothing inside-out that morning, you court bad luck if you fix it. Spilled salt means a fight. Bubbles floating on your tea means money is coming your way.

She also held to "happy the bride the sun shines on; unhappy the bride that the rain rains on." It was snowing when my bride and I left church on our wedding day, January 24, 1953, and my nervous mother was quick to point out that snow was not rain.

But if rain was bad for brides, it was good for caskets. I remember on more than one occasion being a pallbearer and carrying a casket from the church to the hearse in a downpour, trying to take what comfort I could that, even though I was getting soaked, the rain, according to another superstition, was providing a direct path to heaven for the deceased.

To guarantee good weather for an outdoor event, hang a rosary in a tree a few days in advance. Annie Shine Cimini, one of Mae's grandchildren in Boston, recommended that method to a friend who was getting married, telling her by phone that it seemed to be a foolproof system and had worked for the Shines for generations. The friend, not a Catholic, found it all very strange but decided it couldn't hurt.

It rained so hard on the day of the wedding that the bridal party had to detour around flooded streets to get to the church. It turns out the bride-to-be misunderstood the instruction and heard *hosiery* instead of *rosary*. So her mother draped a pair of pantyhose in a tree.

My mother also believed it was good luck for a baby to cry during its baptism. She always instructed us that as godparents we had a moral responsibility to make sure the baby cried during the ritual, even if we had to pinch it, which is what she did when confronted with a placid infant during its baptism, including the kitchen-sink ceremony.

For our part, the Shine boys decided that our mother was also blessed with the gift of precognition—an ability to foresee future events. This was based largely on her own pronouncements. When, for example, the bottom of a soggy bag of garbage fell out while one of us was carrying it across the kitchen, she would look at the sodden mess on the floor and say, "I could have told you that was going to happen."

Stories about ghosts, fairies, banshees, changelings, and post-mortem visitations were part of the culture at our house. A man in Carrick who cursed a priest was rendered blind; another, guilty of the same sin, died a short time after the offense when he fell from a scaffold.

When my mother died, her brother Mike was seriously ill in the hospital. A few hours after Mae's funeral, Mike's wife, Alice, went to visit him. When she walked into the room, Mike told her, "Mae was here. You just missed her. She was wearing that dress I like so much." Because of the seriousness of his own illness, Mike had not been told about his sister's death. The dress he described was the one in which my mother had been laid out. Nobody in the family seriously doubts that she stopped to visit Mike on her way to heaven.

Although Mae believed in the effectiveness of "pishogues," charms or spells that could be summoned to bring luck and protection or to inflict injury or death, she also was wary of them. After my 1954 visit to Carrick, I wrote her about my time there and told her about an incident in Doherty's Pub. I was at the bar with her father when a disheveled, wild-haired woman came into the pub with a child wrapped in a dirty shawl. She was what was then called a tinker, now more commonly referred to as a traveler, or one of the "traveling people."

The woman walked up to James Conlon, pulled the cover away from the child's face, which seemed to have been smeared with soot, and asked him: "Please, sir, something for the baby." She pronounced it *babby*. James Conlon turned to Mrs. Doherty, who was tending bar, and said angrily: "Can't you do something to keep these people out of here?" He then turned to the woman and told her to leave.

With an expression of pure evil on her face, a look I can still see, the woman said, with all the venom she could summon, "Curse ye! The curse of Christ on your black soul! Curse ye to hell!" I remember feeling a distinct chill at the poisonous and deliberate way she spoke the words, not shouting but spitting them out slowly, making sure they had the desired impact.

My mother was clearly bothered when she read about the incident in my letter. She told me later that she wrote her father the day she got my letter to make sure he was well. When I came home a year later from the service, she insisted I go over the incident again and tell her, in precise detail, exactly what had happened, asking me to repeat the woman's words. She was relieved when I assured her that they were not directed at me. When I was dismissive of it all, she told me only the foolhardy took curses like that lightly. Apparently a dictum like "See a white duck, spit for luck" was one thing, but a serious curse was something else entirely.

I confess to being more superstitious than I would like. I have my feet planted firmly in the twenty-first century, I have a bachelor's degree and one semester of graduate school. I am a serious journalist, trained to question everything and to believe that even the most mysterious happenings can be explained reasonably.

But I never put my hat on the bed or new shoes on the table, try never to leave a house by a door other than the one through which I entered, and never, ever stir with a knife, preferring, if a knife is the only other option, to use my finger. I also believe that there are certain strange and curious things that occur, things that defy any attempts to explain them logically.

I suppose I should not find any of this strange since much of the Catholic doctrine in which we were immersed from childhood is replete with words like *mystery* and *mystical*. It provided the fertile soil for this kind of thinking to take root. We were kids who embraced without question the miracles of lepers made clean; blind men who suddenly see; the deaf whose ears were opened; the halt, the lame, and the crippled who take up their beds and walk; the dead who are brought back to life; water into wine; loaves and fishes; walking on water; the mystery of the Trinity; the Virgin birth; and the presence of God's body and blood in consecrated bread and wine. It is probably safe to say that the predisposition to accept the supernatural was infused in Catholic kids at a very early age.

Nor were the nuns at St. Rose reluctant to reinforce it all. The stories were endless. One involved a boy whose arm was paralyzed, frozen in premortem rigor when he struck a priest in anger. After the boy's death a short time later, we were told, his mother had to go to the cemetery each year on the anniversary of the assault because on that day the boy's paralyzed arm pushed through the dirt of his grave. His mother had to use a stick to beat the withered limb until it retreated into the grave for another year.

We were also told that if we were diligent in wearing the brown cloth scapular around our necks and were wearing one when we died, we would be admitted immediately to the Kingdom of Heaven, regardless of what kind of life we had led. The first question that occurred to us, of course, was whether this applied to even the most dedicated sinners who made sure to always wear a scapular and were wearing one when they died. Did they get into heaven, sins and all?

The nuns gave us the answer before we had time to ask the question. They told of a man given to a life of debauchery and licentiousness who always wore a scapular as his hedge against eternal damnation. As he lay on his deathbed, his hand protectively over the scapular he was wearing, he suddenly screamed out in pain, "This thing is burning me!" He tore the scapular from around his neck, threw it on the floor—and promptly died.

Lesson taken.

God's presence in the communion host was also an immutable article of faith. If you were dry-mouthed from fasting since midnight, taking communion almost always caused the host to stick to the roof of your mouth. Trying to dislodge it with your tongue and avoid having it come in contact with your teeth—a violation of church law—was often a perilous exercise. To loosen it with a finger—yet another breach of church doctrine—was a sacrilege beyond comprehension. Always present in our minds was the story the nuns told us of the boy who deliberately bit into the host at communion one morning. We could see him as the nuns described him to us, his eyes bulging in terror, blood trickling from the corners of his paralyzed mouth.

I also remember clearly the morning that a sense of panic swept the small church in Allenton, a town north of Detroit, during the funeral Mass for my wife's grandmother. The altar boy assisting the priest at communion was carrying a paten full of communion hosts when he walked in front of a large electric fan on the altar. In what can only be described as a Eucharistic blizzard, the air around the altar rail was suddenly filled with flying hosts. For a moment it looked to me like the elderly priest was going to faint. But he recovered, dropped to his knees, and began retrieving the hosts. The ushers immediately sealed off the area with folding chairs to keep it uncontaminated until it could be scrubbed with linen cloths. The shaken altar boy stood to one side trying not to cry.

It was against that backdrop, and with all the Irishness that surrounded me thrown in for good measure, that my judicious approach toward all things otherworldly was developed. Nothing in the intervening years has seriously altered it.

In 1962 I wrote a story for the *Free Press* about a family of seven who abandoned their home on Detroit's West Side because of the ghostly presence of an old woman. Her continued appearances in the house finally forced the family to flee in terror one night after dinner, leaving with only what they were wearing. A neighbor called the paper to report the strange goings-on.

I went to the house and went inside, where I saw the unwashed supper dishes still on the kitchen table and pots and pans sitting on the stove. I spent about a minute standing at the doorway, peering into the darkened bedroom where the old woman last appeared, and then quickly left the house. I had stayed just long enough to be able to answer my editor honestly when he asked: "Did you get inside the house?" I was relieved that he did not ask me how long I was inside, which was about five minutes. Maybe less.

Later that evening I located the frightened family at the home of the wife's parents. I talked to the family members about what they had seen, came back to the paper, and wrote the story of the unwanted visitor who became known as "the Horrid Hag of Martin Street."

The story caused a great stir in the city. Calls flooded the *Free Press* switchboard. So many people came to see the house that the police from the nearby McGraw Station had to barricade the street to control traffic. The day-shift officers were held over that evening to help keep the crowds away.

The day the story appeared, Derick Daniels, the city editor, told me it would make a great follow-up story if I were to spend a night in the house and record my experiences for *Free Press* readers. I told him I would rather not. Surprised at my response, he asked, "You don't believe in ghosts, do you?" I told him that I did not have what could be considered a dogmatic belief in all ghosts but I believed in that particular ghost.

Daniels sent Jimmy Pooler, one of the paper's best feature writers, to spend the night in the house. Pooler was not a young man—he had started at the *Free Press* in 1923—and even though he was Irish, he must have decided the possibility of a great story outweighed any concerns he might have harbored about a spectral hag running loose.

Pooler went to the house, but before he could get inside, a group of kids being chased out of the backyard by the police ran into him, knocking him down and breaking his arm. I never told Pooler that I saw it all as some kind of deliberate providential intervention designed to keep him from staying in the house where perhaps something much worse than a broken arm awaited him.

Circumstances that defy explanation weren't limited to stories from the nuns at St. Rose or haunted houses on the West Side of Detroit. On a vacation trip to Italy in 1998, I visited a World War II–era American military cemetery a few miles from the house we had rented in Tuscany. Two of our grandchildren, Ted and Neala Berkowski, were with me, along with their father, Larry. As we walked through the cemetery, the kids ran ahead, up the great expanse of green lawn, between endless rows of white crosses, toward a memorial at the top of a rise. We caught up to them where they had stopped to rest, halfway up the hill. They were sitting on the neatly trimmed grass next to a marble cross that marked the grave of a Michigan soldier, Stanley Grabiec. His surname was the same as that of a Detroit family that had a cottage four doors from us at Stoney Point, Ontario. Although we had lived near them for thirty-five years and were good friends, we had never heard them speak of losing a family member in World War II.

We called Eddie Grabiec and he told us that Stanley was his

older brother, killed in action early in the Italian campaign. He told us none of the family had ever been able to visit the grave. He was stunned at our story of how we came across it.

We returned to the cemetery later that week, brought wildflowers the children had picked, and put them on the grave. We took some pictures and made a charcoal rubbing of the cross and brought them back to Stanley Grabiec's brother and his sister, Helen.

Reasonable people might see the incident as nothing more than a remarkable coincidence. But considering that the cemetery covers seventy acres with 4,402 graves, nothing will ever convince me that the encounter was simply happenstance.

Rules and Regulations

Mae Shine was, as one might expect of a naturalized American citizen, generally respectful of the law and its attendant rules and regulations. As a mother she understood the importance of rules to the maintenance of domestic order.

Her rules were law, and violations of those rules, even marginal ones, were never overlooked. Punishment was swift and summarily dispensed. It was never delayed until my father came home from work. If our house was the domestic version of the British constitutional monarchy, my father was the figurehead monarch and she was both houses of Parliament and the Lord High Executioner.

On the other hand, regulations and prohibitions formulated by others—governments, businesses, property owners—were another story entirely. She considered any regulations or prohibitions that did not work in her favor to be open to wide and liberal interpretation. So she ignored rules she considered frivolous or ones she decided were deliberately designed to confound her or to make her life difficult. She was a master of rationalization and always managed to arrange it so things worked out to her benefit. Her universal response to any posted prohibitions that she was preparing to ignore was usually something like, "What the hell do they know?"

Leaving a downtown Detroit parking garage one night after attending a concert with Sister Irene Kerich, a nun from St. Ambrose, my mother became annoyed at being stuck in the middle of a long line of cars slowly inching toward the exit. When she spotted an open gate and a driveway, she told Sister Irene to drive through it. Sister Irene pointed to the "DO NOT ENTER" sign and the one below it that read, "NOT AN EXIT." Ma recalled telling Sister Irene to ignore the signs, adding, "What are they going to do, put us in jail? An old lady and a nun? Won't that look good in tomorrow's *Free Press*?"

Sister Irene drove past the warning signs, through the open gate—and over the steel spikes that shredded her front tires. My mother, of course, having already decided to ignore the signs, did not bother to read the part that contained the warning that using it as an exit could result in severe tire damage. I have since decided that even if she had read the part about the tire damage, she still would have urged Sister Irene to use the unauthorized exit. She would have considered it a question of calling their bluff.

Among the certainties that dominated Ma's thinking was a profound suspicion of authority and a deep and abiding belief that nothing was on the level. After she died, we found a lifetime of utility receipts stuffed in dresser drawers against the day some gobshite from Detroit Edison would call thirty years after the fact to tell her she had not paid her bill for March 1936, and she would respond instantly, "The hell you say," and dig out the receipt.

I once wrote a column for the *Free Press* on the death of a colorful *Detroit Times* reporter, Joe Umek, noting that his personal philosophy had been "nothing's on the level, not even bass fishing." When Ma read it, she called to tell me how much she liked him, even though they had never met.

One of her favorite maxims was "There's favor in hell." She believed that if you had some influence with the devil, you could probably get a more desirable accommodation in hell than the condemned souls who were hopelessly without connections. A cartoon I saw once in the *New Yorker* showed two naked businessmen relaxing comfortably on lounge chairs in a cavernous setting clearly meant to represent hell. One is reading a newspaper and the other is smoking a cigar. They are being attended by a tailed, horned devil carrying a tray and serving them cocktails. The man with the paper tells his companion: "It's Hell, but at least it's white-collar Hell." I smiled when I saw it, thinking that my mother would have surely seen it less as a comic interlude than as yet one more validation of the way things really work.

One year, while I was a student at the University of Detroit, my father, at my mother's urging, agreed to call a friend who was postmaster of a branch on Chene near Gratiot and ask him to get me a job delivering mail during the Christmas holidays. My father never made the call. He told me, out of my mother's hearing, that I could not go through life expecting people to make calls for me every time I needed a job. Obviously not a subscriber to the "Favor in Hell" approach to employment, he told me to go to the post office branch, ask for a job, and get it on the strength of my own ability, not because somebody made a call for me. If I didn't get it, then there was a valuable lesson in that, as well.

I took the streetcar to the branch, talked to the assistant postmaster, and told him boldly that I wanted a job carrying mail during the holidays. I filled out the application he gave me and left it. I never heard from him. My father said it was a good introductory lesson in the hard-knock ways of the world, much better than if I had been hired only through his intercession. My mother would have seen it all as reinforcement that the system operates on the strength of who you know and that to believe otherwise was foolish and naive, as well as a guarantee of continued unemployment.

I have always suspected that the real reason my father did not make the call was that, like so many others of his generation—especially the Irish—he was not comfortable asking others for help. He was always a proud man, and I'm sure it would have been difficult, maybe even painful, for him to call a friend and ask for a job for his kid.

When I was trying to get the *Free Press* to hire me as a copyboy while I was still in college, the post office experience seemed to be repeating itself. A friend at the University of Detroit, who was a copyboy at the *Detroit News,* told me not to waste my time because most copyboys on Detroit's three daily newspapers got hired because they had relatives or friends working at one of the papers.

Undeterred, I went to the newspaper more than a dozen times to ask for a job and each time was sent away without one. Things eventually reached the point where the editors in charge recognized me as I walked across the city room and sent me on my way even before I had a chance to beg for a job. I must admit I was beginning to see the obvious advantages of the "Favor in Hell" doctrine.

I started showing up at the paper after 6 p.m., on my way home from U of D, after the day-shift editors, who knew me on sight, had gone home. One night in 1950 Charlie Haun, then the night city editor, took the time to ask me where I lived and a few questions about my family and where I was going to school. When I told him U of D, he smiled and said, "Good teachers, the Jesuits."

He also asked me, curiously, if I was Irish. I told him my parents were born in Ireland. He then asked if I would be able to work Saturdays as a copyboy. I told him absolutely. He told me to show up in the city room at 9 a.m. the following Saturday. I did and stayed for forty-six years. When I learned some time later that Haun was hopelessly Irish and had attended the University of Detroit, I wondered if the "Favor in Hell" factor had, in fact, quietly manifested itself that evening.

I think my mother's cynical view of how the world works might have been a condition of growing up in a country colonized by another, a place where the rules were made and enforced by strangers with no real stake in the process. As a result she was always prepared to wage her fight at barricades she established. And there always seemed to be an abundance of barricades.

She considered the shortages of food and certain consumer goods and the subsequent rationing necessitated by World War II to be less an inconvenience than one more challenge to be embraced. Never mind that the inside walls of every store in the neighborhood were plastered with patriotic posters urging all Americans to share the burden. She bartered, traded, finagled, and hustled her way through the war. If she was at all deterred by the reminders

posted in the stores—"RATIONING MEANS A FAIR SHARE FOR ALL"
and "RATIONING SAFEGUARDS YOUR SHARE"—it didn't show. She
was not about to leave the determination of what was her fair share
in the hands of people she didn't know and hence didn't trust. And
she was, thank you very much, perfectly capable of safeguarding
her share without any help from the government.

I am also convinced that if she believed for a moment that the
handsome, grinning young GI looking down from the poster on the
wall behind the counter at Al's Market—urging us to "DO WITH
LESS—SO THEY'LL HAVE ENOUGH!"—was going to have to do with
less because some Irish housewife on Detroit's East Side was trying
to work the system, she would have started growing her own veg-
etables and canning them. She believed, I'm sure, that the military
was quite capable of caring for its own, which was no more than
she was trying to do on the home front.

In truth, the posters with their Madison Avenue versions of the
housewives/mothers and their cookie-cutter perfect children, mostly
blond little girls with pigtails, did little to inspire self-sacrifice. The
models did not even remotely resemble any mother from our neighborhood. They were actress-beautiful, with professionally styled
hair, perfect makeup, and crisp linen aprons tied smartly across
the fronts of their fashionable outfits, not a cotton housedress or a
faded chenille robe in the bunch. They posed in their make-believe,
modern kitchens wearing high-heeled shoes, for God's sake. If the
homemakers of Detroit's East Side were part of the audience that
the propagandists of the Office of War Information were targeting,
they had not even come close.

If my mother's conscience as an American citizen who deeply
loved her adopted country was even mildly troubled by her behavior in those years, she would quickly banish any qualms by pointing
to the cars with "Class X" gasoline stickers on their windshields.
When gasoline rationing was imposed, about a year after Pearl Harbor, the government established classifications for what it decided
was the equitable distribution of fuel.

Drivers in Class A were deemed nonessential drivers and initially limited to three gallons a week. Class B drivers were those—traveling salesmen, for example—who needed their cars to work, and they were allowed a little more. Class C included doctors and law enforcement people; they got more than the A's and B's. But when a special category, Class X, was established for VIPs, politicians, and elected officials, it was positive reinforcement of my mother's basic and long-standing belief that nothing is on the level. Any concerns she might have had about her shadowy wartime pursuits faded quickly as she imagined America's overstuffed politicians motoring off every Sunday for a nice drive in the country with their overstuffed families. That the X category was quickly abolished made no difference to her. She believed that the VIPs would have kept it in place if they could have gotten away with it.

That we did not own a car, and therefore were not allowed a gasoline ration, deprived her of yet another element in her efforts to undo the work of the War Rationing Board, but it did not mean she withheld criticism of the system.

Mae Shine's most valuable currency in those years seemed to be cigarettes, which nobody in our family used. They were in terribly short supply, and she always bought her maximum quota and used them to good advantage. She preferred dealing with the most hopelessly addicted smokers because they seemed the most willing to surrender valuable ration coupons for meat and food staples at an exchange ratio so skewed and so unbalanced that the resulting transactions can most accurately be described as swindling.

"I'll never understand," she would say, standing at the stove, the wonderful smell of frying bacon filling the kitchen, "why these people would rather have a pack of Camels instead of a pound of bacon." In fact, she knew exactly why and never hesitated to take shameful advantage of it.

Among the things we found after her death in the fabled green box was "Individual Beer Ration Coupon Book No. 4069619," issued to her in July 1944 by the Liquor Control Board of Ontario. She was apparently able to acquire it during our three-week summer vacation that year in a rented cottage at Point Pelee, Ontario. Each coupon was good for the purchase of six bottles of Canadian beer, and the book shows that she used the entire allotment of twenty coupons for July and August and five of the September coupons to purchase beer—a total of 150 twelve-ounce bottles. How she managed to use the August and September coupons when our vacation in Canada ended in July remains a mystery. That she was able to find a way to do it is much less mystifying. She could, it seemed, do whatever she made up her mind to do, something that is supported by a lifetime of evidence.

Since my father was not much of a beer drinker and my mother drank no alcohol at all then, something that changed when she discovered the delights of champagne some years later, this was not about acquiring a three-year supply of beer for the Shines. It was about Mae Shine's getting her hands on a valuable supply of precious trade goods. As a result we left Canada that summer with a large quantity of hard-to-get items, especially Heinz ketchup, which was produced in Leamington, Ontario, not far from our cottage. She had made some dark bargain with the Greek proprietor of a diner in Leamington; he got beer and we got fifteen bottles of ketchup. In the United States she would have had to part with eight ration points for a fourteen-ounce bottle of ketchup, so her net gain was 120 ration points. Money, I am convinced, was always an incidental part of the deal.

I had been with Ma earlier that summer of 1944 when she was trying to acquire some ketchup from the same restaurant owner in a cash-only transaction. He brought out four bottles on that occasion, put them on the counter, and told her she could have them for twenty-five cents each. She started to argue with him. Not because she thought the price was not fair—it was—but because paying the asking price sent the signal that you were a pushover, a designation she was unwilling to live with. They argued for fifteen minutes or so until the man, unyielding on the price, snatched up the ketchup bottles and took them back to the kitchen. "He's tough," she said, not without a little admiration, as we left the restaurant without the ketchup. She also learned a valuable lesson that day about the futility of trying to bargain with Greeks. Later that summer, when the beer became a part of the transaction, the discussions turned out to be much more beneficial for both parties.

It is reasonably safe to assume that in addition to the ketchup, she probably smuggled across the border some of the beer, a valuable trade item for her domestic operations, especially with the smokers whose cigarettes always seemed to taste better with a cold beer.

In addition to the beer ration book, the Canadian government also gave her a ration book for food items. In the space on the front of the booklet for the number of people served by the card, someone, in a clumsy bit of forgery, had changed the 5 to a 6. We can only guess that my mother realized some small advantage by increasing the number of people in our family by one.

Sometime between Pearl Harbor and D-Day, a one-hundred-pound sack of sugar turned up in the closet off the front room of our upstairs flat on Lycaste. I don't remember anybody ever talking about where it came from or who dragged it up the steep flight of stairs. We came home from school one day, and it was just there, an imposing burlap bulk leaning against the back wall of the closet, behind the winter coats.

This, of course, freed up Ma's sugar ration coupons—one coupon for one pound of sugar—to be used in furtherance of her questionable wartime activities. So, using a cracked china teacup with a broken handle as a scoop—a damaged relic of some long-forgotten dish night at the East End Theatre—we kept our sugar bowl filled well beyond the surrender of the Axis powers in 1945. The war was over and we still had sugar left. The Allies had their victory, and Mae Shine was still enjoying hers, well into the period of postwar recovery. When sugar rationing was finally ended in June 1947, we had only just begun to scrape the bottom of the burlap.

My mother never met a rule she didn't want to skirt. She balked, for example, at paying full fare on public transit for her obviously over-age kids, considering it a shocking example of age discrimination. She also believed that the rule requiring her sons to start paying the barber the adult rate for haircuts when they turned fourteen to be, by any definition, patently unfair.

She reasoned that at fourteen a boy's head is still smaller than an adult's head and that if the barber is expending less time and energy cutting fewer hairs on the smaller head but charging the same rate as he does for cutting more hairs on a larger head, he is committing nothing less than retail fraud. It all seems very convoluted but it made perfect sense to her. It's the reason I spent as much time as I did sitting in the chair at the Nick and Mack Barber Shop on Jefferson and lying about my age.

I can remember clearly those painful conversations with the barbers.

"Well, Neal, you're now, what, in the ninth grade these days?"

"Seventh," I would lie, feeling the heat rising in my cheeks and trying to disguise my changing voice. I showed up for my children's-rate haircut one day when I was at least eighteen months over the line and a full three or four inches taller than Mr. Nichols, the Nick of the Nick and Mack partnership. He snapped the white bib smartly, tied it at the back of my neck, and then asked: "Shave today or just a haircut?"

It was a watershed moment for me, and I went home that day and told my mother I was finished lying to save fifteen cents on every haircut. She acquiesced but complained for the next year, every time I asked for money for a haircut, about the surplus of chiselers in the world willing to take money from children and lining their pockets with the ill-gotten gains.

Following the end of World War II, Mae Shine regularly visited her family in Ireland. When she did, she brought with her cartons of cigarettes and boxes of cigars in amounts large enough to be considered, by even the loosest legal standard, contraband. She had brothers who were serious smokers and sisters married to smokers, and American cigarettes were a luxury they could not afford. James Conlon enjoyed an occasional cigar and thought the Webster Fancy Tales she brought him could have come straight from heaven.

It is important to mention that she considered customs and excise laws to be nuisances formulated by petty bureaucrats with little else to do but come up with ways to make life difficult for the common people. She considered international laws that interfered with what she believed to be her God-given right to transport consumer goods freely across national frontiers to be no different than the rules the United States was eager to impose on her for the same thing. So she took the global view and ignored them all.

She was always careful to pack the cigarettes and the cigars in the same suitcase. When she arrived at Irish customs, she would look around for the inevitable priest who was coming home to Ireland to visit his family. When she spotted one, she would tell the unsuspecting cleric, in a brogue a bit more pronounced than it had been when she left Detroit the previous day, that God would surely bless him if he would be kind enough to give an old lady a hand with her luggage since she could not manage it all on her own. Then she would hand the bag containing the illegal tobacco products to the priest, who would graciously carry it through customs for her.

I asked her once if she ever worried that the customs inspectors might open the priest's bag and uncover her little smuggling scheme.

"Are you kidding?" she said. "They were always so damn busy tipping their hats and bowing and scraping—'Father this' and 'Father that'—that it would never occur to them in a million years to ask a priest to open his bag."

In 1985, crossing from Canada into Detroit at the Detroit-Windsor Tunnel, I failed to declare two Waterford crystal wineglasses. I had to pay duty on the glasses and was fined $50. All I could think of that day was that my mother would find out and how disappointed she would be at my inept attempt at smuggling.

I never told her.

Another Damned Cowboy Shirt

I was born in 1930, Jim in 1932, and Bill in 1936. During those years my mother suffered a couple of miscarriages, something not discussed until we were adults. At some point my mother decided it was all right to tell us that she believed these were the daughters who were never meant to be.

She talked about walking through the J. L. Hudson department store downtown and looking at girls' dresses, pretty straw bonnets with bright ribbons, patent leather shoes, white anklets, pleated skirts, and little blouses with lace collars, then putting it all down and going to the boys' department to buy, as she once put it, "another damned cowboy shirt."

If she regretted not having any girls, it was not something she made a point of mentioning. But it was always clear to my brothers and me, because of the way she bonded with her three daughters-in-law, whose side she would take in any domestic disagreement, regardless of circumstances. As a result we were careful never to do anything in our marriages that would give Ma the chance to turn on us.

Had she had a girl, Ma undoubtedly would have enrolled her in ballet classes. Her daughter would have been graceful and elegant, light on her feet—every movement fluid and effortless. It would have been, to my mother, a fair reward for her oafish sons. I don't think the Shine boys were any clumsier than other children at the same stages of development, but Ma seemed preoccupied with our every misstep. Having us walk without tripping over ourselves was high on the list of what we saw as the extravagant expectations she had for us. The list included, but was not limited to, good grades, good manners, good grooming, and good posture, except for those times when we were instructed to slouch in order to confound ticket takers and transit workers who would have expected my mother to pay full price if they had even suspected our correct ages.

As a serial stumbler I have painful memories of being repeatedly reminded of my singular ability to find the only available mud puddle on any given outing and fall in it. When my mother decided I was old enough to understand the principle of breech delivery, she explained that I, her firstborn, had been a breech baby, as if it might somehow explain my tendency to regularly fall down for no apparent reason.

"You came into the world arse-backwards," she was fond of reminding me, "and you've been conducting your life accordingly ever since." I took the information less as a troubling reminder of the medical circumstances of my birth than as a quasi-scientific explanation of what seemed to be my disposition toward clumsiness. Given the translation of our original surname, O'Seighin, Irish for "descendant of Seighin, the wild ox," I firmly believed destiny had doomed me to an existence in which disaster was never more than a misstep away.

On a vacation to Austria in 2001 I slipped and fell hard in a hotel shower the first night. A week later, walking down a steep path from an ancient Celtic settlement, I lost my footing and skidded several yards down the mountain on my bottom. I could picture my mother looking down from behind a cloud, smiling and shaking her head. Her awkward kid, still at it after all these years.

Her preoccupation with all this is not buried deeply in the collective psyches of all her sons. In December 2002 we had a small gathering at the home of Bill's daughter Lynne. It was the kind of post-Christmas gathering we had been having since the extended family grew too large for us to have Christmas dinner together without renting a hall. And, as it always seems to, the conversation inevitably turned to Mae Shine and the predictable series of reminiscences that always seem to begin with "Will you ever forget the time she—?" What followed was the usual string of often-outrageous stories of our life with this unusual woman and how her influence still resonates in her children and her grandchildren.

At one point that night it was suggested that, the next year, in lieu of exchanging presents within the family, the children, grandchildren, and great-grandchildren should use the money to buy an engraved brick paver for the new Memorial Walkway at St. Ambrose Church in Grosse Pointe Park, her parish for the last forty years of her life.

The discussion centered on the most appropriate memorial, size, cost, and location. The choices ranged from the small six-by-six-inch stone for a $500 contribution, all the way up to an elegant eighteen-inch diamond-shaped limestone paver for $2,000. A very handsome stone bench that could be appropriately inscribed was available for $2,500.

We quickly decided that if we made the least expensive choice, she would consider it an insult and would, we believed, find a way to visit some unpleasant payback on all of us, even from beyond the grave.

"Why don't we get her a bench?" someone suggested.

"Bad idea," Bill said. "She'd be furious if someone she didn't like came and sat on it. She'd want to be able to control the sitting."

We agreed that this could be a legitimate concern and that we should not do anything that might distract Mae from the pursuit of whatever level of eternal happiness she sought in heaven. A bench, we all agreed, would certainly be a distraction. So we decided to get the largest stone and have it marked as follows:

MARY ELLEN CONLON SHINE

1909–1987

Why don't we, someone then suggested, have it raised a half-inch higher than the other stones and add the words "PICK UP YOUR DAMN FEET!" for the people who will inevitably trip over it?

Bill said that would work only if she were there to say the words herself and smack the stumblers on the back of the head with her open hand as she issued the instruction, which is how she regularly reminded my brothers and me to pick up our damn feet.

That we first thought of the church when thinking of buying something to remember my mother was only natural. The church, whatever its faults—and she never hesitated to point them out in great detail—was an essential part of her life, both in Ireland and America. So, logically, it became part of ours. There was never any question that we would be educated in a Catholic school. Ma believed that we needed to be protected from the snares of irreligiosity that she was convinced lay in wait for the unsuspecting Catholic child in a secular world.

At St. Rose School we were committed to the care of the Sisters, Servants of the Immaculate Heart of Mary (IHM), an order of nuns based in Monroe, Michigan. They were wonderful teachers and serious, but not harsh, disciplinarians. I am still profoundly grateful to them for the guidance that directed me toward a life in journalism.

I am reasonably sure that because I was hopeless in science and math, they believed that whatever small talent I might have had for writing was probably going to be my only hedge against the sobering prospect of joblessness. So they encouraged me to write. Sister Francis Marie gave me permission to do a project on Shakespeare's *Macbeth* in the form of a daily newspaper. I drew and lined an eight-column format and painstakingly lettered in each story, sketching the pictures myself. The lead story bore this headline:

LADY MACBETH QUESTIONED
ABOUT ROLE IN KING'S DEATH

Next to it was my hand-drawn version of a mug shot of the

accused. The caption read: "Lady Macbeth in custody: Out, out damned spot!"

It was a pretty good-looking page and I got an A for the exercise. Years later at the *Free Press,* to accompany a picture of Humane Society officers who were removing a few dozen neglected dogs from the house of an eccentric old woman, I wrote the caption "Out, out damned Spot!" It was rejected by a humorless editor who saw it as too flippant for a story about a poor woman who was losing her beloved pets.

I was also a committed reader of books, and writing seemed to be a natural extension of that interest. A friend of the family, Mrs. LaFortune, never visited us without sitting down to read with me. She was able to teach me to read before I was in the first grade and gave me my first book, a 1929 edition of *A Child's Garden of Verses,* by Robert Louis Stevenson.

My first serious writing (my description) was an unpublished collection of mawkish love poems, heartfelt sonnets I wrote for Patricia Ames, the grade-school girl of my dreams. I did most of that writing by the Detroit River, which provided an abundance of privacy. I wrote the short verses in a spiral notebook with a red cover that bore a drawing of a football player under the words "BIG RED ONE."

I never shared the poems with anyone, especially not Patricia. She might have shown them to her mother, who would have told my mother, who would have had a fit that I had involved that sweet little girl in my libidinous pursuits. And, of course, Ma would have lamented how she would never be able to face Mrs. Ames again without being forced to relive the shame of it all.

When I finished a poem, I would read it over a few times to let the beauty of my rhymes wash over me before ripping the pages from the book, tearing them into small pieces, and scattering the fragments on the iron-gray surface of the river. I learned early in my writing life that moving water is a most forgiving critic. The river accepted my work without comment and carried it gently away, past Belle Isle and Grosse Ile and on toward Lake Erie.

As a child I was also blessed with access to the wonderful language patterns of the Irish, not just in the books I read but also from the people who were part of my life in those years. They were people without an abundance of education, but their love of the spoken word and the richness of their language made a lasting impression. The Irish are, if nothing else, people who would never say something in three words when a dozen would do just as well.

Most Saturday nights they gathered at our upstairs flat on Lycaste. They sat around the kitchen table, played cards, and talked. They also drank a little whiskey, mostly inexpensive blends like Four Roses or Imperial, but every now and then someone, to their delight, would show up with a bottle of what they called "the good gargle," Jameson's or Old Bushmills.

From my bedroom off the kitchen I would listen quietly to their stories, their poems, and their songs. They talked about the place they called home, not about a village or a townland or a parish or a county. Just *home,* a universal designation they all seemed to understand. They talked about the hard life in Ireland. They talked about "the Troubles" and about the Easter Rising and happily revisited their own past treasons, small defiances that grew larger with each telling.

They spoke of the people they had left behind, talking about "our Mick" and "our Kathleen" to set them apart from someone else's Mick or Kathleen. And when they referred to a sudden and tragic end to a life, the person in question was never just killed as much as he was "killed entirely," an element, I am sure, that provided some kind of Irish dimension to the passing.

They would recall the often unrewarded efforts of the Christian Brothers or the Presentation Brothers to educate them. Con O'Sullivan would again tell the story of the day Brother Malachi asked the class, "What is a prince?" and how he hurled his slate at the head of the boy who answered, "Prince is a dog's name." Then they would laugh as loudly as they always did when he told the story.

Before the evening ended, old John Brown would stand up to sing. He always seemed to be wearing the same brown suit coat with shiny elbows, and trousers that did not match. He would tug at the bottom of the jacket, throw his shoulders back, press his fingers on top of the table, clear his throat, and sing "Skibbereen." In his reedy tenor he would sing of a father explaining to his young son why he had left Ireland. It was a story filled with sadness, a story of hunger, eviction, cold, and the death of the boy's young mother in the snow. John Brown, his thin voice trembling with the despair and disappointment of that sad place in that sad time, sang:

Oh, it's well I do remember that bleak December day,
The landlord and the sheriff came to drive us all away.
They set my roof on fire with their demon yellow spleen,
And that's another reason why I left old Skibbereen.

When John Brown finished and sat down, they sat for a few minutes, not talking, before getting up to leave. Then they filed noisily out the door, calls of "God bless" and "Safe home" following them down the narrow stairway. I would try to sleep, my head filled with sad songs and vivid images of rebellion and famine in this land called Ireland, a place I had never seen but a place I knew was part of me.

When I went to Ireland in 1954, I also visited my father's people. On my first night in the small cabin on the farm in Kerry where my father was born, I had a strange feeling about the place. It was not so much a feeling that I had been there before as it was a sense that I belonged there. A friend later told me the experience was something called genetic memory, a feeling of belonging and a sense of being at home in a family place you had never seen before.

But even though I had not seen it, I had heard about it all my life in great, rich detail. The Irish speak English with the kind of lush extravagance that gives life to whatever and whomever they talk about. My father and most of the Irish who passed through our house over the years were remarkable storytellers and, though they had little formal schooling, they were masters of the language and truly "the greatest talkers since the Greeks," as Oscar Wilde once claimed.

I have read of a dark night that was more fully and richly explained by an Irish farmer as "you'd need the eyes of a cat to see the length of your leg on a night like this."

A description of a local fellow might come with the gentle reminder: "Give him tuppence toward a pint and you'll not see his arse for the dust," a colorful reference to the man's affinity for Guinness. The man's return from the pub was inevitably described as "coming out the lane, he was, and not a foot under him," making clear the predictable results of overindulgence without resorting to pejoratives. Sometimes his condition was described simply as being "fluthered" or "destroyed."

My mother's description of people with less than their fair share of intellectual skills was always "thick as a double-ditch." She was also a walking compendium of aphorisms, most of them, it seemed, with futility as the common theme.

Wanting something we obviously could not have brought this response: "Wish on one hand, want on the other," or, "If wishes were horses, beggars would ride." When we expressed disappointment at getting something less than we wanted or expected, she would remind us, "When all fruits fail, welcome haws," a tough thing for American kids to comprehend, especially ones who did not know what haws were. When I finally looked it up in the dictionary and learned that it was the fruit of the hawthorn, I also had to look up *hawthorn*. I don't think they were indigenous to Detroit.

When ordinary food seemed extraordinarily tasty, Ma would explain that "hunger is sweet sauce." Anticipating any kind of hopeful but unlikely outcome for ourselves was met with "when the sky falls we'll all catch larks."

Growing up surrounded by Irish entailed some small drawbacks as well. When my brothers and I were enrolled at St. Rose, we spoke English with a brogue, which delighted the sisters, most of whom were of Irish heritage. But I also remember being embarrassed after relating to the class one day that Jesus "made the blind man see and the deef man hear." Sister Coletta gently corrected me. That night I asked my father which was correct, *deaf* or *deef*.

"Deef," he told me, and went back to his newspaper. I decided the prudent course was to stick with deaf, even if it was wrong. Sister Coletta also told me the letter H was not pronounced "haitch."

One day in religion class Tommy Stundon, whose parents were from Kerry, described Judas Iscariot as an "eejit." At that time, I think, nuns were forbidden by church law to laugh out loud. So they turned their backs on the class, faced the blackboard, and trembled until the moment passed. This particular moment, I recall, took much longer than usual to pass. Thinking about it today, I have decided that "hoor's get" would have been a more appropriate description of Judas, but the Stundons were a proper family and it would never occur to Tommy to use language like that in school.

I also remember dodging a potentially embarrassing moment the day our class was discussing the discovery of America. A color drawing in our history book showed two Native Americans standing on a bluff, arms crossed, watching stoically as the three ships of Christopher Columbus sailed toward shore. It was a well-known picture, the Indians each wearing an elaborate feather headdress with colorful blankets draped over their shoulders.

When the question was asked about what the picture portrayed, I raised my hand and waved it wildly, hoping to get called on. I was eager to tell the class that the name of the taller Indian was Gilhooley. My father had seen me studying the book at home and told me about Gilhooley. He was, my father said, a descendant of one of the sailors who was with Brendan, the Irish saint, who was the first to discover America, doing it about a thousand years before Columbus and his "Eyetalians" showed up. Ethnic rivalries being what they were in our neighborhood, we were always happy to have any kind of advantage over the non-Irish kids at St. Rose. The sailor stayed to make a life in America, my father explained, like so many of the Irish since that time. Gilhooley was the chief of all the Indians in America when Columbus arrived, my father said, pointing out proudly our long and impressive history of running the country.

I did not get called on, and my mother told me the truth when I expressed my disappointment at not being able to share the Gilhooley information with my classmates, especially with Aldo Cardosi.

If reading and writing were my perceived scholastic strengths, arithmetic was a threatening and discouraging counterbalance. A report card from the ninth grade, found in the green box, shows an impressive consistency in my arithmetic grades. That the course was now being called mathematics had no noticeable influence on my pitiful efforts to conquer it. A number by any other name is still a number. I got a D on each quarterly marking, a D on the final exam, and a D for the final grade. It should be noted in my favor that I converted an incomplete in the third marking period to a full D by completing the missed assignments, an indication that one can be an academic disaster but a conscientious student.

A more tangible example of how basic numeric concepts elude me can be found on the pages of a "spiritual bouquet" that I prepared for Mother's Day 1940, when I was nine. It too was found in the green box.

A spiritual bouquet was an inexpensive but touching way to honor someone you loved on special days. The church provided small folding cards, the outside covers of which were appropriately adorned with a color lithograph of the Blessed Virgin, and they listed the various spiritual opportunities available with which to honor your mother: Masses, Holy Communions, visits to the Blessed Sacrament, rosaries, Our Fathers, Hail Marys, and ejaculations. An ejaculation was any one of a series of very short prayers—exclamations, really—that could be said silently and in impressive numbers.

Opposite each of the spiritual bouquet categories was a line on which the giver could fill in the number of prayers, Masses, communions, rosaries, visits, and ejaculations he or she was willing to offer for the intentions of the person to whom it was presented. The higher the numbers, of course, the stronger the indication of the level of regard in which the benefactor held the beneficiary.

My favorite ejaculation was "My Lord and My God," and I figured I could knock off a few hundred of them just on the way home from school. The problem with ejaculations was keeping any kind of accurate count. "My Lord and My God—one, My Lord and My God—two, My Lord and My God—three" worked only to a certain point before the little prayers and their cumulative totals got hopelessly jumbled. I relied heavily on estimates.

Visits to the Blessed Sacrament were also easy obligations to fulfill. We were never told that these visits had to be anything more than just showing up—no prayers, no pause for devout reflection, no time requirement. Maybe it all went without saying, but in our religious lives nothing went without saying. Either the visits to the Blessed Sacrament came with specific guidelines or all of it was open to personal interpretation.

So a visit to the Blessed Sacrament consisted of cutting through St. Rose Church after school on the way to the St. Rose Sweet Shop—in the east door, executing a gliding genuflection as you hurried past the tabernacle, out the west door, and across Beniteau to the soda fountain. Repeating the process in reverse on the way home counted as another. We also decided that in fulfilling the pledge to attend Mass, we automatically got credit for a visit, a kind of spiritual bonus.

In the 1940 Mother's Day spiritual bouquet, I promised to receive Holy Communion seven times and to attend Mass five times. Since even people with only a rudimentary understanding of the sacred rites of the Church of Rome knew that Holy Communion had to be taken during Mass, I no longer try to understand how I failed to comprehend that it was impossible to go to communion seven times at five Masses. I can only plead that then, as now, numbers turned my mind to pudding. I could, of course, have received communion at two subsequent Masses to fulfill the pledge, but that would have meant not getting spiritual bouquet credit for those Masses, a waste of two perfectly good Masses.

I signed Jim's name to the card, as well as my own, but it was clear who did the arithmetic.

When it came to spiritual bouquets, the temptation was always to overcommit. Thirty Hail Marys when twenty would have sufficed, fifteen rosaries when ten would have worked just as well. The good sisters reminded us of the importance of not promising more than we were prepared to deliver and made sure we understood that once promised, the burden to fulfill that promise was a serious one. But they never mentioned a specific spiritual penalty that attached to failure to deliver, something that did not go unnoticed by some of us. It was apparently not even a small sin if, in a rush of religious enthusiasm and prodded by the depth of your love for your mother, you promised more than you could possibly deliver or, worse yet, than you ever intended to deliver.

Also, there was no expiration date. No limited time frame in which you were required to fulfill your pledge before it was nullified. I am convinced that the open-endedness of it all was my ultimate undoing. I am a journeyman procrastinator—the nuns of IHM called it "dilly-dallying"—and have always been deadline driven. No firm end date for the project, no serious chance of my ever finishing it.

That is why, along with the apparent absence of any defined penalty for nonperformance, I estimate that my long-term spiritual bouquet indebtedness runs well into the thousands. It's not that I went into it all fraudulently. My heart was generally in the right place. But even as I was inflating the numbers to make sure my mother understood how profoundly I loved her, reality was whispering in my ear, "You're never going to be able to do all this." I knew it then and know it now as I continue to rely on the existence of some little-known canonical statute of limitations on all I owe.

In 1940 I appear to have taken, perhaps out of concern for my mounting spiritual bouquet debt, what can only be described as a minimalist approach to the spiritual bouquet movement. In addition to embarrassingly small numbers for all the categories—a departure from my standard practice—I pledged on that occasion—and I still can't believe it—one ejaculation.

What could I have been thinking? Every kid knew the ejaculation was the pushover category of the spiritual bouquet. Any dope could rattle off one "My Lord and My God" every second. So how can I explain my decision to put down one? I can only imagine, more than sixty-five years later, that on Mother's Day in 1940 I penciled in the number one and simply forgot to add the zeros. I have already explained my problem with numbers.

The following Easter I apparently came to my senses. In a spiritual bouquet for my mother and father, I promised 15 Masses, 15 Holy Communions, 30 visits to the Blessed Sacrament, 15 rosaries, and 1,600 ejaculations.

My perennial problems with math have had all sorts of ramifications in my life. In the winter of 1952 my mother was looking forward to my graduation from U of D later that year as a kind of minor miracle as well as a reaffirmation of her belief in the power of prayer. The Selective Service System, on the other hand, was eagerly anticipating the expiration of my student draft deferment, so I decided to outfox my draft board and become a naval officer. We were still at war in Korea, and the U.S. Navy looked to me like a safer alternative than being drafted into the army and stuck in the infantry because, as far as I was able to determine, the conduct of the Korean War had yet to involve any major naval engagements. I also thought the naval officers' uniforms were pretty snappy.

The navy had recently dropped its college trigonometry requirement for officer candidates, something that certainly would have disqualified me as an applicant, although a multiplication tables requirement also would have doomed me.

I signed up, underwent an extensive interview, and was given a date for a written test involving math and verbal skills. I asked my girlfriend, the aforementioned Phyllis Knowles, by this time an executive secretary at Continental Aviation, if she would tutor me for the math portion of the exam. She had been an all-A student, giving some measure of truth to the theory that opposites attract.

When I showed up at her house for the first session, she had all her math books assembled. "Okay," she began, "we can skip fractions, right? You do know fractions, don't you?"

"I don't know fractions," I confessed sheepishly. So we started with fractions, and over the next few weeks we worked our way through algebra and geometry until she thought I had a reasonable chance of squeezing through a simple math test. I passed. I did well enough on the written and verbal portions to elevate my overall score just beyond a passing grade.

Several weeks later I got a letter from the Navy Department denying my application. It cited "a lack of technical subjects through college." It should have been clear to me in the beginning that a branch of service that had until recently required college trigonometry as a condition of admission was not seriously interested in having an officer in the wardroom of a heavy cruiser who was conversant in nineteenth-century American poets.

The army inducted me on May 11, 1953, put me in the Medical Service Corps as a private, and in November sent me to Austria. I left behind Phyllis, to whom I was married in January 1953, and our four-day-old daughter, Judith Ann. We had moved in with my parents when I got drafted.

At that same time my mother was busy with her own numerical exercise. She was quietly counting the months and days between our marriage, on January 24, and Judy's eventual birth on November 14, nine months and twenty-one days later.

Looking back at my academic efforts during my years at St. Rose, if I had one quarrel with the IHM nuns in those years, it was their unwavering belief that every one of their students, even those of us with less than a full allotment of native intelligence, was always capable of better work. It was, of course, a philosophy to which my mother fully subscribed.

She fussed endlessly over my grades and begged me to tell her why I was not doing the kind of work of which I was, by IHM dictum, clearly capable. She told me tearfully of how she hated to go shopping because of her humiliation when meeting the mothers of my classmates and listening to them boast about the academic success of their children, all of whom seemed to be exceeding my demonstrated capabilities.

I protested that I was working as hard as I could in school and perhaps the painful truth was that I was not capable of better work. I told her that perhaps God, in his infinite wisdom, had decided the world would be an exceedingly boring place if every child were an honor roll student. So, I argued, he added a few C students to the mix to keep things interesting. Anyway, I told her, I considered myself a "strong C" student and urged her to relax and not mess with God's obvious plan.

Of course, she bought none of it, insisting that the nuns at St. Rose were actually in a better position than God to determine the kind of work of which I was or was not capable. When I offered to do her shopping so she would be spared the indignity of meeting the mothers of smarter children, she looked like she wanted to hit me but had decided not to, probably because I was in high school.

She told me one afternoon, during a particularly painful discussion of another substandard report card, that if I made the honor roll just once, "just to show me that you can do it," she promised she would never again carry on about my scholarly shortcomings. I fell for it.

I was in the twelfth grade, and the next term I worked harder than I had ever worked on school assignments. I did extra reading, spent time in the public library gathering information from reference works, and raised my hand every time a question was asked in class, even when I didn't know the answer. I rejected my standard practice of going through my finished essays to add adjectives and adverbs to raise the word count on papers where I had failed to meet the required minimum. Now, on papers that required five hundred words, I wrote a thousand. Overnight I turned myself into a giant of learning. I became a scholastic juggernaut. I made the honor roll.

When I brought the certificate home and proudly handed it to my mother, she looked at it for a moment and said crisply, "If you can do it once, you can do it every time." Instead of letting up about my grades, she increased the pressure. I never made the honor roll again. She never stopped lamenting my failure to use the gifts God and the IHMs had given me. And I never stopped asking myself how I could ever have been naive enough to believe her in the first place.

My father's expectations of scholarship in his sons were as high as Ma's, but he was not as committed as she seemed to be to push us toward better grades or complain about bad grades. I can remember that he would look over my shoulder while I did my arithmetic homework, which usually involved long intervals on my part while I waited, often in vain, for an answer to come into my head so I could commit it to paper. While I sat, pencil poised, he would watch for a while before walking away shaking his head.

When my classmates at St. Rose elected me president of our graduating class in 1948, my father conceded that I was certainly affable but, as a scholar, still hopeless.

The most outstanding example of how deep this "capable of better work" philosophy ran in the IHM order came about forty years after I graduated from St. Rose. Phyllis and I were visiting Sister Miriam Therese at the IHM Mother House in Monroe. She had been our homeroom teacher during our senior years at St. Rose, mine in 1948, Phyllis's in 1950.

During our visit Sister Miriam Therese mentioned a column I had written two weeks earlier for the *Detroit Free Press*'s *Sunday Magazine*. It was a tongue-in-cheek exercise based on President and Mrs. Clinton's habit of accepting invitations to spend vacation time at the grand summer homes of rich Democrats. In the column I offered the First Family the opportunity to spend a quiet weekend at my summer cottage in Stoney Point, Ontario, with its three tiny bedrooms and one small septic tank.

She told me she considered the column a weak effort that read like something I had thrown together at the last minute with little advance thought.

"It was not," she told me, "your best work."

It was, in fact, a disturbingly accurate assessment of that particular column, but I was defensive nonetheless. I told her some people, especially my neighbors in Stoney Point, had found it quite humorous. She looked at me over the top of her glasses and asked, "How many of them?"

On the way home I told Phyllis that I could not believe that forty years later, Sister Miriam Therese was still picking my writing apart.

Phyllis turned to me and said: "Maybe we all still need someone in our lives to keep reminding us that we are capable of better work."

But it was Sister Miriam Therese who got me a copy of the course catalog for the U of D and gave it to me in the months before my 1948 graduation from St. Rose. She had marked the pages containing the required courses for a bachelor's degree in journalism. The following September my friend and classmate Larry Keegan and I took the Jefferson streetcar to U of D's Dowling Hall on Jefferson and St. Antoine and enrolled. I graduated four years later with a degree in journalism, Larry with a degree in business.

During my college years my mother continued her harangue about my failure to get better grades and her disappointment in me, especially because everybody knew I was capable of better work.

When the university later gave me its Tower Award as an outstanding alumnus, honored me with its President's Cabinet Award, and conferred on me an honorary PhD, designating me a "doctor of humane letters," nobody involved ever mentioned my grade point average. My mother, had she lived to see it all, would have said scornfully, "How soon they forget."

It was another of the nuns at St. Rose, Sister Marie Loretta, who first suggested to my mother that I try out for one of the school's dramatic productions, sending me down yet another perilous path that I had theretofore been reluctant to travel. Sister Marie Loretta told me she wanted me to read for the lead role in the Stephen Foster musical the school was producing. Instead of being flattered, I was terrified.

In those years I tended heavily toward shyness—something I have since managed to overcome—and I was frightened beyond description at the thought of appearing before an audience to do anything. Today medical science has a name for it—social anxiety disorder. Back then my mother had her own word for socially anxious people like me: mopes. It was, to be sure, several levels above the dreaded "mollycoddle" designation, but it carried its own special stigma.

She worried that my lack of self-assurance was an unmistakable symptom of mopery, and she was prepared to do whatever was necessary to prevent that. Having me stand on the stage of St. Rose Hall in front of a full house singing "I Dream of Jeanie with the Light Brown Hair" seemed to her to be a definite step in the right direction.

She often admonished me for being afraid to take a chance. Being "backward," she called it, an oblique reference perhaps to the circumstance of my birth. She admired kids who were, in her words, "proper chancers." But I was not a risk taker. I was a committed follower. One of my mother's regular complaints about my character was that I was "easily led."

I was never the first swimmer to dive in the canal, never the first to swing from the fire escape ladder on the Michigan Bell building at Hillger and Kercheval, never the first to tug the rope and ring the big bell at St. Spyridon's Greek Orthodox Church. But I always led the pack as we fled down Kercheval, the bearded priest, his cassock flying, in hot pursuit.

Had I been aware then of the adage "It's the second mouse that gets the cheese," I would have embraced it. Instead, I was renowned, in neighborhood parlance, as a "goal sticker," the kid who was always reluctant to stray too far from the safety of the goal in games of tag or hide-and-seek.

So I brought the Stephen Foster script home and studied it every night. It was, to be honest, a less than demanding role, and the opportunity to croon "Beautiful Dreamer" while holding Shirley Dyer's hand and looking into her eyes had more than a little appeal for me. In my rich childhood fantasies I imagined myself singing, my voice sweet and clear,

Beautiful dreamer wake unto me,
Starlight and dewdrops are waiting for thee;
Sounds of the rude world heard in the day,
Lull'd by the moonlight have all pass'd away!

while Shirley melted at the beauty of it all.

But even though the production had more music than dialogue, in the rehearsals I was never able to get past the first line of the opening scene. I was supposed to sweep into a crowded drawing room wearing a snappy green velvet smoking jacket and exclaim to those assembled, "It does my poor heart good to see all my dear friends here tonight."

But it always came out, "It does my dear heart good to see all my poor friends here tonight." I kept getting it wrong until it was clear to everybody that I was not born to the role. Frankie Willard, my classmate, ended up playing Stephen Foster to rave reviews. I was consigned to the minstrel chorus, without Shirley Dyer, my face blackened with burnt cork, banging a tambourine with the rest of the mopes singing "Camptown Races." I have never felt the same about Stephen Foster's music.

My mother was disappointed but not discouraged by this theatrical setback. She knew I would probably give the Christmas pageant another shot. I was a regular at the tryouts for the pageant. Actually, they weren't really tryouts. We were ordered to show up, and everybody was required to participate at some level. There was a good selection of male roles in the Christmas play, and the dialogue was even less demanding than Stephen Foster's. In the previous pageants I had no real success in landing a serious role. I always ended up as a shepherd. It was a lot like being a minstrel, except that at least the minstrels got to sing. Shepherding was silently servile. To tell the truth, I still think convent politics had a lot to do with who got what roles.

All that aside, the truth was that I desperately did not want to be a shepherd again. The shepherds were the lost souls of the Christmas pageant, leftovers from a casting process that had no foundation in equity. We were a swarm of nameless urchins condemned to wander the papier-mâché hills of Judea in tattered bathrobes and old tea towels, unrecognized and forsaken except by parents like my mother who, though they loved us, had no real appreciation for the lonely and ignominious existence of the stage shepherd.

As Advent progressed, I worried that the lingering disappointment of my failure to land the Stephen Foster part would be compounded if I once again was assigned a role no more demanding than tending the flock of painted and chipped plaster sheep that Mr. Holscher, the custodian, hauled up from the church basement every December to be used in the pageant before being consigned to the crèche on the side altar of the church.

On the day the assignments were made, I prayed to whoever happened to be on prayer duty in heaven that I be delivered from the apparently inevitable lowly pastoral duties. I do not need to be Joseph, I prayed, trying not to make my request too extravagant. One of the wise men would do very nicely, the innkeeper, perhaps, or even the herald angel, whose lines I had memorized from years of listening to them being directed at me and my sheep-herding cohorts as we feigned drowsiness.

But when the selection process was completed and somebody else had been chosen to play Joseph opposite Patricia Ames, always a shoo-in for the part of Mary, and the wise men were already busy selecting their colorful robes, and the herald angel was on the way home to have the rips in his oversize wings stitched by his mother, I knew the gloomy inevitability of the next line.

"And the rest of you will be the shepherds."

As shepherds we were required to supply our own costumes. In addition to getting out the old bathrobes, we converted threadbare castoffs from the basement ragbag—mostly bath towels and dishtowels—into makeshift headdresses, burnooses, kaffiyehs, djellabas, and turbans (there never seemed to be a serious preoccupation with historic authenticity in wardrobe selection). The use of its towels as costumes in a religious pageant was obviously not something Cannon Mills had in mind when it produced these items decades earlier for use in America's bathrooms and kitchens.

It was to be my last year as a career shepherd, and in a way it was a noteworthy final performance. Because of my years of experience I had attained senior shepherd status, adding a new dimension to the level of my participation in that year's Christmas panorama. Like everything else in life, the shepherding game had its own societal pecking order.

I was selected to be the shepherd who—in exaggerated pantomime—passed the good news of Christ's birth to the other shepherds piled in simulated sleep on what seemed like every inch of the stage in St. Rose Hall. As I passed among them, rousing them from their counterfeit slumber, I managed to step on several, including one surly shepherd who complained loudly enough to be heard in the back of the hall. The audience laughed. The nuns did not. My mother understood that none of it was really my fault, that it was a condition of my birth. Whatever the reason, my days on the stage were blessedly at an end.

My missteps in the Christmas pageant notwithstanding, my recollection is that my brothers and I were not particularly troublesome children and, could not, by any fair measure, be considered a burden to our mother. That she hit us from time to time, even when the reasons seemed unclear, was an accepted part of growing up at a time, and in a neighborhood, where the maternal imperative included smacking your kids when they clearly had it coming—or at least when the mother decided they clearly had it coming. When we complained that we had been whacked for something a brother had done, she told us to consider it payment for a time when we had done something wrong and had escaped punishment. It would, she reasoned, all balance out in the long run.

She made sure we understood that the principle of certainty of punishment meant that every domestic transgression carried its own set of penalties and that the chances of avoiding them were never part of the equation. She believed that justice deferred was justice delayed, so violations of the rules resulted in an immediate rush to judgment, followed quickly by the appropriate punishment, most often corporal. Our constitutional right to a speedy trial was never in jeopardy, although the appeals process left much to be desired.

In situations in which it was not clear who was at fault, she hit us all, confident that the real culprit got what was coming to him, collateral damage to the innocent notwithstanding.

Even being injured did not stop Mae Shine from the swift and resolute distribution of punishment. In the early 1940s she slipped and fell on the stairs of the S. S. Kresge store downtown and broke her pelvis. She took the Jefferson streetcar home and the next day took the bus to the office of Dr. Clarence Williams, our family doctor. He sent her to the hospital.

When she was released she was confined to bed for a couple of weeks, which meant she lacked the ability to come after us for behaving badly. We had to go to her. She ordered the designated miscreants to her bedside, where they were smacked and dismissed. When she was ambulatory once more, she maintained order by hitting us with her crutch.

Of the three boys, Jim was clearly the most accident prone. In the first ten or twelve years of his life he was knocked down at least five times by automobiles. Whenever we ran across the street in traffic, Jim always seemed to be the one who didn't quite make it to the other side.

His first encounter came on our way to school one morning. Jim was in the first grade and I was in the third. The policeman had stopped all the cars on Jefferson at Beniteau—all but one. Jim ran into the street and was sent flying. I waited until the police ambulance took him off to Receiving Hospital and then went on to school. I knew Jim was already in trouble for getting hit by a car. I was not interested in getting into trouble for not going to school. I had a clear mental picture of how it would go if I went home.

My mother would ask, "Why aren't you in school?"

"Jim got hit by a car."

"Don't change the subject. Why aren't you in school?"

I decided that going to school was my safest option. Wrong decision. I got yelled at for not coming home to tell my mother that Jim had been hit by a car. It was my first experience with a no-win situation.

Jim's arm was broken. It would turn out to be his most serious auto-related injury. He never suffered anything more serious than cuts, scrapes, and bruises in his subsequent car-hits-boy incidents. But one day Rita McFarlane, a childhood playmate and neighbor, knocked on our door and told my mother, "Jimmy got hit by a car."

"How bad is he hurt?" my mother asked.

"I think he's dead," Rita answered solemnly.

Jimmy had, indeed, been knocked unconscious by the car and was not moving when Rita saw him. By the time my mother got to the scene, Jimmy was sitting in the streetcar tracks on Lycaste in front of the Conovers' house, next to the car that had hit him.

Jim remembers what happened: "She ran up to me, stood me up, looked me over from top to bottom, and when it was clear to her that I was not dead, not even dying, she smacked me and sent me home."

It was certainly not an unexpected reaction. When I was ten or eleven, I fell through the ice in the Detroit River. My brother Jim, a friend named Ray Mowid, and I had decided the river looked solid enough for us to cross to the east end of Belle Isle, which looked enticingly close. As the oldest, I volunteered, uncharacteristically, to take the lead and test the ice.

Winter or summer, the river was a constant attraction. We lived about two blocks from its banks and saw it not as any kind of hazard but as something put there by God as a great place for us to play. We understood, in some kind of abstract way, that it could be dangerous. Even when Walter Collins, a classmate, drowned in the river, it lost none of its allure. If we even heard the warnings of "Stay away from the river!" that our mothers shouted as we ran off to play each day, they went unheeded.

We were about halfway to the island, and I was shuffling gingerly along the uneven ice, pressing suspicious patches with the toe of my galosh, when I heard what sounded like a car door being slammed. The ice suddenly gave way under me, and I plunged in up to my armpits. I held on to the ragged edge of the ice as my galoshes filled with water, and I could feel my legs being dragged by the river's current.

I was howling when Jim and Ray ran to the edge of the hole, grabbed me by the arms, and pulled me out. Why all three of us were not swept to our deaths that morning still confounds me.

I don't remember telling my brother and Ray Mowid not to take me home that day. Nor do I remember either of them suggesting that I needed to go home. It seemed to be a simple, unwritten precept among kids that the last person you want to see when you are plucked from an icy hole in the river is your mother.

I suppose it would seem reasonable to reasonable people that a child in a situation like that would hurry home, tearfully explain what happened, and be comforted by the hugs and kisses of a mother grateful that her child had not been swept to an icy death in the unforgiving waters of the Detroit River. I knew that, in my case, the possibility of that scenario was nonexistent.

The most likely outcome was that—after a determination had been made that I had suffered no harmful effects from the incident—I was going to get popped several times for disobeying (we were forbidden to ever go near the river for any reason), ruining a perfectly good pair of pants (my school corduroys), and nearly drowning my brother and our playmate. Also, nearly drowning someone who was not a blood relative carried its own unique social burden. Mae Shine's unspoken concern would most probably have been, "How will I ever be able to face Mrs. Mowid again?"

I was still weeping loudly when we reached the Mowids' house, two or three blocks from the river. My galoshes were still filled with water, and my pants had started to freeze by the time Jim and Ray, one on each arm, led me quietly down to the basement. Ray's parents, Fred and Eva, were not home. They were probably next door, working in the small grocery store they owned.

I stood shivering in my underwear next to the open door of the coal furnace next to the chair on which I had hung my pants until I was dry enough to go home, about two or three hours later.

We were probably correct in assuming that if I had gone straight home, frozen and penitent, my mother's response to the situation would have been exactly as I expected. We would also have been safe in assuming that this response would have been acceptable to the other mothers in the neighborhood. The collective approach to child care in that community in those years was impressively uniform.

While my mother's relationship with my brothers and me could be, at times, less than affable, she had a cordial relationship with the neighborhood kids. They were always welcome at our house, where they could expect to be fed if they were around during mealtime, and she never did anything that would designate her as a crab.

Her standing was reinforced one afternoon when a group of St. Rose boys showed up at the parish hall to play basketball. The ladies of the Altar Society were still cleaning up after their weekly luncheon when the basketball began bouncing. Mrs. Matte, doyenne of the St. Rose Hall kitchen, came out of the kitchen and told them to leave and come back later. She said the hall would be closed until after the ladies were finished. As the unhappy players slouched, grumbling, toward the door, one suggested, loud enough to be heard by Mrs. Matte, "Why don't you all go home and cook the old man a decent meal for a change?" By the time Mrs. Matte hurried out of the kitchen to see who had made the offensive remark, the offender was already running up Kercheval Avenue.

Mrs. Matte turned to the women in the kitchen, who had also

heard the comment, and asked angrily, "Did anybody see who that brazen boy was?" They all said no, including my mother, who had seen the brazen boy and knew he was Richard Conover, who lived down the street from us on Lycaste. She could hardly wait to get home that afternoon to tell us what had happened, laughing while she told the story. She also admitted that Richard's remark about decent meals had some deeper truth, making it clear, of course, that none of it applied to her.

The next day we saw to it that word got out in the neighborhood that our mother had refused to fink on Richard. Her reputation as a noncrab was stronger than ever.

After my father's death she supplemented her income by tending children, most often teenagers, while their parents were away. She genuinely loved young people, although the parents might not have been entirely happy if they knew that she taught many of them to play poker, including one obscure variation—"Youngstown Sheet and Tube"—that involved a lot of wild cards, including "one-eyed jacks and the king with the axe." It was an adaptation, she said, that was popular in United Auto Workers union halls. She never told us where she learned it.

The kids she took care of loved her, but I am convinced their parents might not have shared the sentiment if they had a fuller understanding of her philosophy of child care. She believed, for example, that forcing teenagers to go to church was an empty exercise that produced no substantial religious benefit.

One scrupulously Catholic family always told her to make sure their teenage children went to Sunday Mass while they were in her care. She told the kids they could go to church if they wanted to or stay home. It was their choice. She said if they decided to stay home, one of them needed to stop by the church, pick up a copy of that Sunday's church bulletin, and leave it on the table where the parents would see it. She said she did not encourage them to lie, just to let the parents reach the obvious conclusion on their own. When we told her once that she was walking on shaky moral ground, she told us to either show her our degree in sacred theology or shut up.

One of the women whose children she sometimes cared for could be charitably described as thrifty. My mother called her a tightwad. On one occasion the woman took Mae Shine to the freezer to show her the meat to be used for meals while she and her husband were gone. "Lots of hamburger, a package of hot dogs, and some round steak," my mother remembered. Tucked behind those designated offerings my mother spotted a box of prime steaks. When the family returned a week later, most of the hamburger was still frozen. The steaks were gone.

"The kids loved it," she said.

She even gave two of the frozen steaks to the cleaning lady to take home. "I told her to be sure not to thank her [the lady of the house] for them."

One of her charges, Tracy Gormley, a high school student, was old enough to drive, but her parents told my mother that Tracy was not allowed to use the car while they were away. When Tracy begged my mother one morning to let her take the car to school, my mother told her: "Take it if you want to, but if your parents find out, I'm going to say you stole it." Tracy decided against taking it.

Our oldest child, Judy, remembers the card games she and her siblings learned from their grandmother when she took care of them, at her house or at ours.

"We always needed something to bet with during the poker games," Judy said, "so we used chocolate chips or toothpicks, whichever was handy." After an evening of card playing in which everybody in the game had ample opportunity to handle the chocolate chips or the toothpicks, they were put away.

"Grandma would scoop them up and put them back in the bags they came in," Judy said, presumably saved for the day they would next be needed, either for another card game or for something closer to the use for which they were originally intended.

"I think she taught half the kids in Grosse Pointe how to play poker," Judy said.

Her poker tutorials weren't the only evidence that our kids had one of the coolest grandmothers around. She went one night with some teenagers she babysat to see the stage production of the Who's rock opera *Tommy*. Her friends thought she had taken leave of her senses. She told them all they didn't know what they were missing. When I asked what it was like, she smiled and said, "It sure as hell wasn't Guy Lombardo."

Judy also recalls another highlight of being cared for by their grandmother when the grandkids were younger: watching *The Lawrence Welk Show*.

"We drank ginger ale out of parfait dishes, pretending it was champagne, and we drank toasts to everything and everyone we could think of. We loved it. It made us feel very grown up."

Peggy, the youngest of the Shine girls and the second youngest child, has a different memory.

"I used to sleep in the room with the murals," she said, "and I was always scared." When we moved into the house on Wayburn in 1948, the walls of the front upstairs bedroom were decorated with gloomy pastoral scenes painted in dark greens and blues, dominated by a cheerless castle. For a long time, Peggy said, she was convinced that Grandma Shine was a witch lurking somewhere in the old castle.

"I truly believed that if I looked behind her couch, which I never did, I'd see her broom there," Peggy said.

The boys, Jim, Tom, and Dan, remember her relaxed approach to mealtime. If she made spaghetti one day, she always made enough sauce so she could serve it the next day on hamburger buns and call them "Sloppy Joe" sandwiches, they said. The boys say they called this meal "spaghetti on a bun."

When taking care of our children—or Jim's or Bill's—she worked diligently at making sure the older ones did not pick on the younger ones—a skill she developed with her own children, however ineffective it might have been.

Because Bill was the youngest, sibling tradition required that Jim and I spend a lot of time making his life miserable. We played practical jokes whenever we could and teased him mercilessly, mostly because we had to take him with us everywhere we went.

In our makeshift snow forts the cry "Fire at Will!" was—contrary to its accepted military use—the universal order for everybody to throw snowballs at Bill.

(When we were together in Ireland in 2004, the three of us ended up sharing a room at a hotel near Shannon Airport. When I pointed out that it was the first time since we were kids that we had shared a bedroom, Jim said, "Makes me feel like we should be pounding on Bill.")

On the days we ran off to the playground to play baseball, Bill would stand howling on the curb—he wasn't allowed to cross the street alone—until my mother opened a window and ordered us to take him with us. One problem with having him in tow was that he would not pee in the bushes like every other boy in America. When he had to go, one of us had to take him home so he could use the bathroom.

One winter he got new mittens, and after an afternoon of playing in the snow, the dye from the wet mittens had stained his hands purple. "Purple Fever," we told him gravely when he showed us his hands. We said it was a condition peculiar to budding young arsonists and was brought on by his habit of playing with matches, the Jefferson Inn blaze being a case in point. We told him there was no cure for the affliction and that it was always fatal. We told him he was going to die.

He tried, without success, to scrub off the dye and then went crying to our mother, who swatted Jim and me and told us to quit teasing him. Bill was feeling much better because she had assured him he was not going to die.

She's your mother, we told him later. She has to tell you that. She doesn't want to tell you the truth because she knows it will make you sad. But you're really going to die. It was worth the second smacking we got just to hear him howling again.

Bill still says he has never been more convinced of anything than he was when he believed he was going to die that winter of Purple Fever. Even when the dye eventually faded and disappeared and he was still alive, he believed that he had somehow been miraculously cured, not that we had been lying to him.

Our most effective effort at keeping him from following us to the playground and interrupting our ball game by needing to pee came on a Good Friday afternoon. We were ready to go and play ball. Bill, with his tiny bladder, was ready to come with us when Jim and I announced we were going to have a passion play in honor of the Easter holiday.

"Who wants to be Jesus?" I asked. Jim raised his hand and so did Bill. We picked Bill.

Most of the backyards in those years had clothes poles, stout poles anchored in the ground with cross-members with hooks to which the clotheslines were attached for outdoor drying. We got a wooden box and stood Bill on it. We tied his feet to the pole and tied his outstretched arms to the cross-member with pieces of clothesline. Then we mocked him and cuffed him a few times, explaining that it was important for him to understand some of the torment Jesus had suffered.

We told him we were leaving but would be back in three hours to take him down and that we would complete this important religious tableau Sunday morning with his glorious resurrection from beneath the dining room table, which we would turn into a makeshift tomb by draping blankets over it. He seemed to like the idea.

When my mother heard him screaming about an hour later, she looked down to see him strung up on the clothes pole and took him down from the cross two hours early. When Jim and I got home and found the cross empty, we knew that Bill had probably not been carried to his tomb ahead of schedule. We also understood there was a good chance we might be headed to our own tombs in time for Easter. Our explanation, that we were simply trying to provide Bill with the opportunity to understand his faith from an important new perspective by letting him experience it personally, did not sell. We were punished and sent to our room for the rest of the day.

The next morning we told Bill that we considered his behavior—crying after only an hour on the cross—hardly Christlike. We told him he was a disappointment to us and a disgrace to his religion. Because of all that, we said, the resurrection was being canceled. He was clearly disappointed.

Lest it sound like my mother spent most of her time knocking her children around, it is only fair to her memory to point out that none of it was ever serious. No cuts, bruises, or broken bones. No involvement by the police or any agencies responsible for the protection of children. No lingering damage to our psyches.

Bill called it "more symbolic than anything else," a tangible demonstration of her unhappiness with our behavior without ever really hurting us. We learned to dodge, feint, and lean away from her swing, and it never occurred to us ever to say to her: "That didn't hurt." We knew she was probably capable of hurting us, and we were not willing to tempt her.

By relating a lesson learned at his mother's knee, Bill once stunned a group of command officers during a police management training session designed to improve interpersonal relations. The trainer, a woman, had explained that most of life's important lessons are learned in childhood, lessons learned from our mothers. When the trainer asked the group, "What is the most important lesson you learned from your mother?" Bill was the first to answer.

"How to take a punch," he said.

In fact, she never punched, always used her open hand, mostly to the back of the head while we were fleeing. Never in the face. Glancing blows seemed to be her specialty, and when she connected, it was never quite hard enough to hurt a lot but always hard enough to make the point. That she was required to make her point so often can only be laid at the feet of her kids, who seemed to provoke her regularly.

But through it all she was our devoted protector, the mother of the tribe, our lady of perpetual help incarnate. She surrounded us with love and made sure we always understood just how much we were loved.

Once I saw a picture in a history book of a group of sculptured goddesses, called caryatids, that were supporting the roof of an ancient Greek temple. I decided right away that they must all be mothers who, like our own mother, were determined to keep life's frail roof—and the woes of the world—from collapsing on the heads of their children.

Mae Shine truly believed that all of us, as children of the same God, were created equal. She made sure we understood that.

One day, during the civil rights turmoil of the 1960s, she was shopping on Jefferson when the heel of her shoe broke. She hobbled two blocks, to the shoe repair shop she always used, to have it fixed. While the shoemaker was fixing her heel, he lamented the sad state of race relations in the country and told her that if we weren't careful, pretty soon "they" were going to be running things. Then, he said ominously, pointing his finger at her for emphasis, we would be the ones standing in the street and lifting our hats while "they" walked on the sidewalk.

She stood up, took her broken shoe out of his hand, and told him that if we did, indeed, have to stand in the street while they used the sidewalk, she hoped we would be able to accept this new status with the same patience and dignity as they had for the past two hundred years.

She reminded him that both of them, as immigrants, were in this country because those who were born here had graciously allowed them to come and live among them. Let's hope, she said, that when "they" are running things in this country, they don't decide to send "us" back where we came from.

Then she took her broken shoe and walked home in her stocking feet.

Around that same time I came home from work one Sunday night, made a sandwich, and turned on the eleven o'clock news. Bob Maher, from Channel 7, was at St. Ambrose Church interviewing parishioners after Mass. He told viewers that the pastor, Monsignor Lawrence "Scotty" Graven, had distributed during the Mass what he called "covenant cards." The cards said simply that the signer believed in the premise that all people have the right to live, work, and raise and educate their children in the community they choose. The monsignor asked his parishioners to take the cards home, sign them, bring them back to church the following Sunday, and place them in the collection basket.

Before I had a chance to take the first bite of my sandwich, my mother's face filled the screen. Maher introduced her by name, describing her as a long-standing member of the parish. He asked her if she was going to sign the covenant card.

"I didn't even take one," she said.

He asked her why not.

"This is the United States," she said, "and nobody needs my permission or anybody else's permission to live, work, or go to school where they want. We are all children of God, and nobody needs to have a handful of signed cards before they can move on your block, get a job in your neighborhood, or enroll their child in your school.

"Every Sunday," she said, pointing over her shoulder, "this church is filled with people trying to find Christ in there but who cannot see him in their own neighbor. I think that is all very sad."

The next night somebody dumped a bag of garbage on her lawn.

She told me later that she was pretty sure she knew who it was. I asked her whether she was going to leave it on the man's porch that night. She said she was not.

"I'm going to pray for him," she said.

While Ma was bothered that the church as a whole did not respond strongly and vigorously enough in addressing the basic social problems that beset cities like Detroit, she was still a serious Catholic who enthusiastically welcomed the changes of Vatican II. Her devotion to the church did not soften her criticism of it or its designated representatives when she felt it was warranted, something that extended even to the content of Sunday sermons.

Following Sunday Mass at St. Ambrose church, the celebrant could often expect a quick and sometimes biting critique of that morning's homily.

"That was a waste of a perfectly good hour," she told Father Ed Wojdyla as she walked past him outside church after Mass one Sunday. He suggested politely that she might want to make better use of the hour, perhaps by praying. "I can pray at home," she said. "I come here for a little inspiration," suggesting that she found it impossible to find even a spark of it in that morning's homily.

She had little patience with priests who dished out what she considered prepackaged "fail-safe" sermons on grace, good works, sin, redemption, and the eternal rewards of spirituality instead of dealing with the more pressing social issues of the day. "Kissing off" the homily is what she called it.

One Sunday morning Phyllis and I were leaving church after the last Mass, and Father Wojdyla asked me, "Do you know what your mother called me this morning?" I told him I didn't really think I wanted to know the answer. He told me anyway.

"A bastard," he said.

"Isn't that a sin?" I asked sheepishly.

"A very big sin," he said, trying not to show how much he was enjoying it all.

He told me that he had read my column earlier that morning in the *Free Press* and suggested from the altar that those members of the congregation who thought they knew the real Ma Shine, which was probably most of them, should go home after Mass and read what her son had written about her. It could provide, he said, a valuable new insight to what they already knew—or suspected—about her.

He was standing in front of church, he said, when she walked past quickly, an artificial smile on her lips, and, without looking at him, whispered harshly out of the side of her mouth: "I'll get you for that, you bastard."

She had, in fact, already called me that morning about the column. She woke me up at 7:30 to tell me, in a fury, that she was going to sue me for slander.

"I'm tired," she said, "of opening my *Free Press* every Sunday and seeing you put my personal business out there for everybody to see."

I had written that morning about her starring role in the legendary and historic 1937 standoff on our front porch at 635 Beniteau with two men from Crowley's department store and a court bailiff who had come to repossess our furniture.

I told her she could not sue me for writing what was true. She told me she was going to sue me anyway, just to teach me a lesson. Then she hung up, went to Mass, and afterward felt compelled to question the legitimacy of her pastor's birth.

She and Father Ed were, in truth, dear friends, although he once told me that if he had a parish full of Mae Shines, he would seriously consider becoming a monk, living out his days in quiet contemplation in some cloistered abbey in the hills of Appalachia.

When I told my mother about his comment, she said, "Well, he damn well better learn how to bake fruitcakes because that's how those places make their money." She said contemplation might be good for the soul, but as far as she could tell, it didn't provide much in the way of revenue. She was always fond of saying, "Words alone won't feed the friars," her way of telling us that it takes more than talk—even if you're as good a talker as the monks—to put food on the table. It was something we never quite understood since we always thought she was saying *fryers*.

Also, she might have had some insight into Father Ed's lack of cooking skills because she regularly filled in at St. Ambrose on days the rectory cook was unavailable. On one memorable occasion a new parish secretary called Ma the day before her turn with a list of menu items suggested by the priests. Ma interrupted the woman in mid-menu. "Tell them they'll get what I damn well make them," she said. And they did.

Despite her devotion to the Catholic Church, its clergy always seemed to consider it the prudent course to be a bit wary of her. Father Tim Pelc was the relatively new pastor at St. Ambrose when he conducted the Scripture service the night before her funeral. But, new or not, he was familiar with Mae Shine's reputation.

He stood in the front of the crowded room at the Verheyden Funeral Home, paused, cleared his throat, and said, "This makes me very nervous," indicating the closed casket behind him. "I keep thinking I'm going to hear this voice asking, 'Who is this horse's ass?'"

The Shines

My father, Patrick Joseph Shine, was born on May 26, 1890, on a farm in Gurtdromosilihy, Kilbaha, County Kerry, Ireland, near the town of Newtownsandes and about six miles from Listowel. He was the sixth of nine children born to Cornelius Shine, after whom I am named, and Ellen Mulvihill.

Newtownsandes was named after the Sandes family, the local landlord. During the land war of 1886–87, George Sandes, who was both landlord and land agent, was so thoroughly disliked by the local populace that residents changed the name of the town to Newtown Dillon, after John Dillon, a leader of the Land League. Dillon was active in calling for a "No Rent Manifesto" urging Irish tenant farmers to withhold rent from the landlords. The new name did not catch on, and in 1916 it was changed to Newtown Clarke, after Thomas J. Clarke, a leader of the Easter Rebellion that year who was later executed by the British for his part in the uprising. Newtown Clarke did not stick either, and in 1939 the local priest changed it to its present name, Moyvane—Maigh Mhean in Irish, which means "Middle Plain."

But I still remember that all the mail that left from our house, long after 1939, was addressed to Newtownsandes and the postmark on the return mail carried the same name. When my wife and I visited Moyvane in 1978, at least one road sign showed the direction and distance to Newtownsandes. When I asked a cousin why nothing had been done to reflect the forty-year-old name change, he said that it would not be right to pull down a perfectly good sign, and besides, he said, everybody knows that Newtownsandes means Moyvane. The sign, he said, would wear out in its own good time and then they could replace it with one that said Moyvane. Although that old sign was eventually replaced, not everybody has made the transition. The 2004 Michelin road map of Ireland lists the town as "Newtown Sandes." The map of Ireland that the Dan Dooley car rental company provides to its customers shows it as "Newtown Saddles," and the GeoCenter Euro-Map of Ireland calls it "Newton Sandes." The 2002 census of the Republic of Ireland still lists it as Newtownsandes and records its population as 326.

Pat Shine immigrated to the United States in 1910. Because ownership of the farm would pass to his brother, John, who was ten years older, Pat knew his future lay somewhere beyond the rocky hills of Kerry. He joined his two older sisters, Mary and Kate, who were married and living in Pittsburgh. He worked as a laborer in the Jones & Laughlin Steel Mill for a time and then became a locomotive fireman on the company's Monongahela Connecting Railway, which was called the Mon Con. But the work wasn't steady and, in 1914, he and his brother Mike moved to Detroit because a friend told them the city's streetcar company was hiring. Mike was two years younger than Pat and had come to Pittsburgh from Ireland in 1912. According to family legend, Mike had a ticket to sail on the *Titanic* but changed it at the last minute when a woman in Newtownsandes asked him to delay his departure for a few months so he could accompany the woman's daughter, who was immigrating to the United States.

The Shine brothers went to work for the Detroit United Railway, a privately owned transit company that was later taken over by the City of Detroit to become the Department of Street Railways (D.S.R.). Pat Shine was a conductor, Mike a motorman. They worked the streetcars in Detroit until they retired nearly forty years later.

When the United States entered World War I in 1917, they enlisted in the army. Both served in France with the American Expeditionary Force and when the war ended returned to their jobs in Detroit.

My mother was five years old when my father started with the streetcar company in Detroit. Fifteen years later she would get on his streetcar on her way to her housekeeping job and fall in love with him, unconcerned by the nearly twenty-year difference in their ages. To most of the Irish of that generation, it was an acceptable gap.

According to her, however, it was not love at first sight. Her interest in the beginning, she said, was more economic than romantic. On that first day, when she answered his "good morning" in an unmistakable Irish brogue and reached out to drop her five cents in the fare box, he put his hand over the opening and indicated that she should continue through without paying. She was delighted.

So every morning she would wait for his streetcar and would not board until she was sure her Irish benefactor was sitting behind the fare box.

"After all," she would tell us, "a nickel was a lot of money in those days."

One day he asked her to go to a dance with him. She accepted. After a brief courtship they were married on June 29, 1929, in St. Charles Church on Detroit's East Side. Mike Shine was the best man, the notorious Annie Riley, the maid of honor. The bride was twenty, the groom thirty-nine.

To my brothers and me our parents' marriage seemed rigidly formal. Pat Shine was a thoughtful and considerate husband, and I cannot recall him ever raising his voice to my mother. He remembered special occasions like birthdays, anniversaries, and holidays with appropriate gifts, but he was not someone we would look to as a romantic role model.

Two pieces of correspondence from Pat Shine to Mae Conlon survive from 1929, consciously consigned by her to the green box. One letter and a penny postcard provide some insight into his obvious reluctance to allow himself to be swept away by reckless affection.

The letter is directed to "Dear Friend Mae." Written in February, he told her he had called the family for whom she had been keeping house, only to learn that she had scarlet fever and was quarantined in her rooming house at 1780 Townsend. He bragged that he could have violated the quarantine to see her because, as an army medic at a base hospital in France during the war, he had been exposed regularly to contagious diseases and never got sick. "As far as I'm concerned," he wrote, "I am not the least afraid of scarlet fever."

In closing he wrote: "Well, Mae, tho you did not ask me for any money, I am giving you this twenty. You probably can use it now, and if you need any more in the meantime, don't forget to let me know."

When we first read the letter, my brothers and I were properly impressed, calculating that $20 probably represented his salary for at least two weeks. Then we read the rest of the letter: "You can pay it back whenever you are ready. I won't be in any hurry."

He signed it, "With Best Wishes, P. J. Shine, 11002 E. Jefferson," his address at the Truax Hotel on Jefferson and Lillibridge.

The following April he sent her a postcard from a hospital where he was confined with scarlet fever, his self-proclaimed immunity apparently having failed him. His ardor had clearly increased in the months since the $20 letter. This card opens simply, "Dearest." He tells her how terrible it is to be confined, how he had to smuggle the card out to be mailed to her, and agonizes at the prospect of "three more weeks of this." Then, in what for him represented a burst of romantic fervor, he tells her, "Nothing makes me feel better than to hear from you every day. Better by far than a tonic." He quickly shattered the mood by adding, on the same line, "Would you please try and bring me out a toothbrush, 1 doz. Gillette blades and a tweezers for pulling hair." There was no room on the card for a signature.

My brothers and I have decided that she bought the toiletries he requested with what was left of the $20 he had sent her, which was, we are certain, as close as he ever came to getting any of it back.

At no point during the courtship of Mary Ellen Conlon and Pat Shine did my mother meet Aunt Mary, my father's oldest sister. It was not an accidental oversight. Aunt Mary was married to Tom Weir and they lived in Pittsburgh. She was the matriarch of the Shines in America, standing in for their mother, Ellen Mulvihill Shine, still in residence at the farm in Kerry.

My mother already knew that over the years Mike Shine had taken more than one prospective bride to Pittsburgh to be presented to Aunt Mary for approval. All had come up wanting. Aunt Mary's idea of a suitable bride seemed to center mainly on girth. The heftier, she believed, the healthier. My mother often said Aunt Mary's idea of the perfect bride was a woman who was "beef to the heels, like a Mullingar heifer." Uncle Mike apparently never got the message.

"She's a lovely girl, Mike, but she's awful skinny," Aunt Mary would tell him privately when he presented yet one more scrawny young woman for Aunt Mary's appraisal. "Marry her if you want," she'd sigh, "but I guarantee you'll be getting a doctor bill, not a wife." So Mike and the failed candidate would return to Detroit by train, and Mike would end the relationship, usually before they reached Union Depot.

My mother was five-feet-four and not quite one hundred pounds or, as she described herself, "skinny as a stick." She was not even close to the bridal standard. So she never made the trip to Pittsburgh. Whenever a visit was proposed, she found an excuse to avoid going. Too tired. No time. Not feeling well. Unable to miss work. She was, it is clear, not willing to take her chances with Aunt Mary. She managed to delay the inevitable confrontation until after she was safely married.

But even with the Aunt Mary situation in hand, it appeared that another potential impediment to her marriage was manifesting itself in Ireland.

My father's older brother Donal, a former religious brother with the Presentation Order, was making plans to go to Carrick-on-Shannon to meet the Conlons. Mae Conlon may have avoided the confrontation with Aunt Mary about my mother's physical fitness for marriage, but now Donal Shine would determine whether the Conlon family was sufficiently pious.

Uncle Donal was an imposing figure: tall, always well tailored, with iron-gray hair and a striking profile. He taught the Irish language at a National School in Sligo. He was an Irish speaker and believed that all employees of the Irish government, regardless of the level, should be required to speak the language of the country fluently. He was deeply distressed that Irish was not spoken all the time by everyone in Ireland.

When Ireland gained its independence from England in 1922, Irish became the official language. Ireland's 2002 census showed that 43 percent of the population—about 1.57 million people aged three and older—claimed to speak Irish. Of that number, about 339,120—mostly schoolchildren—said they spoke the language on a daily basis. But only about 78,700 adults, out of a population of four million, said they used the language every day.

Uncle Donal made a nuisance of himself by addressing police officers, mail carriers, and other civil servants in Irish, and he would scold—often to the point of embarrassment—those who were unable to respond at a fluency level he considered appropriate. When he felt he had made his point, he followed it with a lecture, in English, about the shameful decline of the language of saints and scholars, the mother tongue of the Irish race.

I met him for the first time on my visit to Ireland in 1954 and found him to be exceedingly proper when it came to manners and behavior. He visited us in Detroit in the 1960s, and the intervening years had not diminished his strong sense of propriety. My mother, always more direct than the rest of us, called him a tight-ass.

My mother's youngest brother, Seamus, remembers the day Uncle Donal showed up in Carrick: "I was about ten at the time. And we got the word—my mother and father got a letter or something from him telling them that he would like to pay us a visit. And he came up on the train from Sligo, which is only about thirty-five miles.

"We saw this guy coming out the Priest Lane, a very stately looking man with a hard hat and a rolled umbrella. He knew his brother had met this girl from Carrick-on-Shannon in America and was going to marry her, and he came up to see what kind of stock she came from."

Seamus said Uncle Donal and James Conlon, not surprisingly, got along wonderfully, with Donal especially impressed with the Conlons' steadfast devotion to the family rosary.

"He found a good solid family," Seamus said, "and he saw all the religious accoutrements around, you know, the Sacred Heart lamp and the big statue of the Sacred Heart, and he obviously went away from there with a good impression."

With no further evaluations to be dealt with, the marriage took place as scheduled. The wedding reception was held in the house my parents had rented at 2147 Drexel, also on the East Side. The party effectively ended when a guest got carried away during a spirited Irish reel, sailed through the front-room window, and crashed onto the porch in a shower of broken glass.

The police were called, and the dancer was taken to the hospital. The bride fainted and had to be carried upstairs to her bedroom, presumably by the groom. She always maintained that she feigned her wedding-night swoon to hasten an end to the party, which she said threatened to go on all night.

It was, to be sure, an Irish beginning.

For many of my years at the *Detroit Free Press*, the painter in the Free Press Building was Ray Mulligan, who was fond of reminding me that he had been a guest at my parents' wedding. He insisted he was not the errant dancer and said that, in fact, he was in the bathroom when the man went through the window and always regretted missing the highlight of the evening. His most detailed description of the reception was always: "It sure was one heck of a party."

Pat Shine and the skinny Conlon girl from Carrick stayed married for forty years, until my father's death in 1969. Aunt Mary quickly came to terms with the marriage, and she and my mother became great friends. Mae Shine did her part by adding a few dozen pounds over the years. Jack Brosnan, one of my classmates at St. Rose, told me when we were in high school that my mother was built like Doc Blanchard, a 208-pound All-American fullback for the Army football team in the 1940s, and I knew Aunt Mary would have been pleased. When I reported Jack's comments to my mother, all she would say was, "Jack Brosnan needs to go home and take a look at his own mother."

Mike remained a bachelor, apparently never meeting an ample girl he fancied enough to marry. He spent most of his life on Detroit's West Side in a gloomy boardinghouse on West Lafayette near Junction, home to a collection of card-playing Irish bachelors, most of them streetcar men.

Every Thanksgiving, Christmas, and Easter, Uncle Mike would turn up at our house for dinner with three or four of these friends in tow, and he would pass out silver dollars to my brothers and me while comparing my mother's cooking, not always favorably, with the food served at Ashley's Restaurant on Fort Street, his restaurant of choice.

He lived with us for a few months in 1952 while he recuperated from a badly broken leg. He had been injured when his streetcar collided with a truck.

The highlight of his stay came during the first week when he bought us our first television set, a handsome RCA floor model with a rich wood cabinet. He was an enthusiastic fan of Gillette's Friday-night fights and was not prepared to recuperate in any setting where he was unable to watch them.

For our part, we had despaired of ever getting a television set. My father believed television was a fad, something that would never catch on. My mother told us he had said the same thing about radio. He apparently felt the same way about automobiles. We never owned one. He often said that if God had wanted us to drive cars, he would not have given us streetcars.

When Uncle Mike was not watching the fights, he sat in a large easy chair reading newspapers and filling the front room with clouds of blue smoke from his R. G. Dun cigars. He kept his plastered leg propped on a white Naugahyde hassock, a piece of furniture clearly not designed for the load. Long after he left, it bore the concave reminder of the plaster cast.

He was in his chair, wreathed in smoke, leg propped, on the afternoon that I introduced him to Phyllis Knowles, my unofficial (no ring) fiancée. What followed undoubtedly was an echo of his experiences in Pittsburgh many years before.

Although Phyllis was standing next to me, Uncle Mike directed his questions to me alone.

"Is she Irish?" he asked.

"No," I answered.

Pause.

"Where are her people from?"

"Her mother was born in Belgium, and her father was born in England."

"Is she a Catholic?"

"Yes."

He paused again for a minute and took a deep pull on his R. G. Dun panatela and looked at us both. In what I am convinced he considered a most magnanimous and high-minded gesture, he said: "Well, I suppose in this country it's probably a good idea to mix the races. I wish you both the best."

When, out of his earshot, Phyllis protested vigorously that she was the same race as I was, I told her not to ever bother to try to explain any of that to Uncle Mike.

"To him there's the Irish race and then there's everybody else," I said, "and nothing will ever convince him otherwise."

He came to the wedding, had a good time, and presented us with a most generous gift of $50. It was, I told Phyllis later, his tangible acknowledgment that he believed we were going to have a good marriage despite our racial dissimilarities. Our six children have taken the mix even further, strengthening the bloodlines with strains of Dutch, German, Polish, and Texan.

Uncle Mike was sixty-six when he died in December 1958 at the

Veterans Hospital in Allen Park. At his wake in Terry McGovern's funeral home, in the shadow of Holy Redeemer Church at West Vernor and Junction, two of the failed bridal candidates from his past turned up to mourn his passing. They were robust and healthy, mothers of large families, still wondering, perhaps, what had gone wrong in Pittsburgh so many years earlier.

Aunt Mary, like her brother Donal, held closely to the family's rigid standards of decorum. All this became painfully clear on the day of Uncle Mike's funeral. I was embarrassed beyond words. My mother thought it was hilarious.

I was assigned to drive Aunt Mary and my father, the two closest relatives, in the car behind the hearse. My mother rode with us, as did Phyllis. My car was a lumbering gray 1953 Oldsmobile sedan, with substantial amounts of rust, a taillight held in place by a pound of Bondo, and a compression problem that made it impossible to restart for at least fifteen minutes after the engine had been turned off. It also had a right front tire that leaked.

On the morning in question I stopped at a gas station on the way to the funeral home to add several pounds of air beyond the recommended capacity to the soft tire. During the Requiem Mass I prayed alternately for the repose of Uncle Mike's soul and that my leaking tire would hold up.

Before we pulled away from Ste. Anne's after the Mass, I surreptitiously kicked the tire. It felt mushy. I started praying again. I had already guessed that Aunt Mary was less than delighted at having to ride to the cemetery in a rusted-out Olds. A flat tire would be a disaster beyond imagining.

The burial was in Holy Sepulchre Cemetery, in Southfield, about twenty miles from the church. I pulled into traffic behind the hearse while the rest of the procession fell in behind me. Twenty minutes into the trip I felt the steering wheel pulling toward the bad tire. I told my passengers that I was going to have to stop to fill it with air. I heard Aunt Mary exhale loudly.

Terry McGovern, the funeral director, was known in the neighborhood as "Terrible Terry," after a well-known prizefighter of another era, "Terrible Terry McGovern, the Brooklyn Terror." Our Terrible Terry was riding in the hearse with the driver, and I had to sound my horn several times to get his attention. Aunt Mary, meanwhile, was making exasperated noises in the backseat.

McGovern leaned out the window of the hearse. I signaled to him that my tire was low and pointed to the Standard Oil gas station ahead of us. He pulled the hearse into the station, across the hose that rang a bell to signal the attendant, and stopped next to the overhead doors near the grease rack.

The attendant heard the bell and came out. When he saw the hearse, he stood for a minute, a puzzled expression on his face, and then removed his hat in a gesture of respect. I apologized and told him I had a low tire and needed air. Behind me the first three or four cars of the cortege had already pulled up the driveway into the station. The rest of the procession was strung out behind us along Grand River Avenue, disrupting traffic.

I pulled over to the air hose, and the attendant rushed to inflate my tire, still bareheaded and looking perplexed at what was happening around him. I dared not look in my mirror at those in the backseat. I could hear Aunt Mary sighing loudly. I knew my mother's face would be red by now from trying to keep from laughing.

I thanked the man profusely, apologized for my intrusion. He said I was welcome, that he was happy to be of help, and told me he was sorry for our loss. I thanked him again and blew the horn. Terry McGovern waved back and the hearse continued on toward the cemetery. In my rearview mirror I watched the entire procession, headlights glowing, moving up the gas station driveway, over the signal hose, past the pumps and the service bays, down the other driveway, and out again onto Grand River. The attendant, his hat now over his heart, stood respectfully at attention as the few dozen cars drove slowly through his station, each triggering the bell as it went. Two blocks from the station I could still hear the faint music of the bells.

Aunt Mary did not say much the rest of the way to the cemetery, but she managed to arrange a ride home with someone else, which was probably a good thing. We had to stop twice more for air on the way home.

While life with Mae Shine was a series of adventures, incidents that perhaps didn't seem funny at the time but became part of family lore over the years, growing up with Pat Shine was decidedly more proper.

He was what fathers were supposed to be—strong, reliable, hardworking, God-fearing; a solid example to his children. He was scrupulously honest. Whatever passengers left on his streetcar, he turned in, no matter how insignificant the item. If the item was not claimed in thirty days, it was returned to him. As a result the Shines became the owners of the most impressive collection of used umbrellas in the neighborhood.

(The first long book I can ever remember reading, *Anthony Adverse,* by Hervey Allen, had been left on his streetcar and not claimed.)

Pat Shine obeyed the law, followed the rules, always crossed the street at the corner, and did not spit on the sidewalk like so many other fathers in the neighborhood. After serving in France in the First World War, he served his country closer to home in the Second—as an air raid warden in the neighborhood. Pity the Axis sympathizer who left his lights on during an air raid drill after Pat Shine had ordered loudly, "Lights out!"

During the last two years of World War II, my mother worked at the nearby Continental Motors factory, a job that Tom McKenna, our longtime boarder who by this time was president of the plant's unionized workforce, helped her to get. "Favor in Hell" was still at work.

Continental supplied parts for military aircraft, and my mother worked on what was called "the burr bench," grinding the imperfections off machined parts. Wearing dark blue slacks and a matching work shirt, her hair tucked into a net on the back of her cap, she took the short streetcar ride to Continental every day. My recollection is that she liked the work, liked the give-and-take of the factory floor, and liked making new friends. Several nights a week some of these new friends showed up for dinner. They were invariably young and from the South—mostly Kentucky and Tennessee. "Just kids," far from home and lonely, is how she would describe them.

The one I remember most clearly is a young blond woman who stayed on long into the evenings, talking quietly at the kitchen table with my mother while this nosy Shine boy eavesdropped from the bedroom. She was pregnant, unmarried, and frightened. I remember her repeating, through her tears, "If you play with fire [she pronounced it *far*], you get burnt."

My mother eventually convinced her that she needed to go back home to have her baby, which I think is what she eventually did. I was never sure, however, what comfort the woman might have taken from my mother's insistence that her situation was far from being a tragedy. The prevailing example of this logic was my mother's frequent declaration that "some of the best families in Detroit got started this way."

The only other memorable dinner guest from the factory was a young man who one night brought with him a gift for the family. It was a cold-cream jar filled with a dark, strong-smelling salve he called possum grease. It was effective, he said, in treating a long list of ailments, including cuts, bruises, scrapes, rashes, boils, blisters, pimples, sunburn, poison ivy, and chest colds. We never tried it, but my mother kept it for years on a shelf in the bathroom medicine cabinet. It was, after all, a gift, and it is a breach of basic good manners to throw away a gift.

She had most of her pay at Continental converted to war bonds. I remember the day my parents took the certificates out of the dresser drawer, counted them on the dining room table in the Lycaste flat, and announced happily that we had enough money for a down payment on a house. We were going to move—away from the Chrysler plant, away from the alley, away from the earthly delights of the Jefferson Inn.

In 1948, after ten years in the upstairs flat on Lycaste, when I was a freshman at U of D, we bought a house at 1119 Wayburn, in Grosse Pointe Park. It was the first—and only—house we ever owned. It was 1.9 miles and a thousand light-years from the Lycaste house.

The house, a two-story brick bungalow on a pleasant street, was perfect. It cost $10,500 and had four bedrooms, two baths, and a large front porch shaded by a canvas awning with wide green stripes. An added selling point was the presence, four doors away, of our parents' dear friends Margaret and Joe Poisson, parents of Peachy of the coal shovel incident.

It was in the section known as "the Cabbage Patch," an other-side-of-the-tracks putdown for our piece of an otherwise fashionable suburb. The area suited Mae Shine perfectly. Being fashionable never seemed to be one of her goals.

There was, however, one serious impediment to the move. My father was a city employee, required by city ordinance to live in Detroit. My mother saw the requirement as an infringement on the constitutional right of Americans to live wherever they wanted, and she decided we should ignore it. My father, a dedicated follower of the rules, decided we should not. The dilemma was resolved when the real estate agent pointed out that Wayburn was the westernmost street in Grosse Pointe Park and the rear portion of the house and lot were actually in Detroit. Because of that, he said, the owner of the house would be paying some taxes to Detroit.

But my father would not buy the house until he had cleared it with the city. After a predictable bureaucratic runaround that lasted several weeks, the city told him he could live at the Grosse Pointe Park address as long as he slept in the part of the house that was on the Detroit side of the boundary. My mother thought this was an even greater assault on the Constitution than the residency law.

But until his retirement four years later, Pat Shine slept alone in the back bedroom. He believed we were nothing if not a nation of laws, even if that meant sleeping in the smallest and least desirable bedroom in the house. My mother thought it was all nuts. "What are they going to do?" she asked. "Come around every night at bedtime and peek in the windows to see where everybody is sleeping?"

Jim, Bill, and I lived in the house until we married, and my mother was living there when she died in 1987. Sometime during those years the boundaries were redrawn, putting the house and lot entirely in Grosse Pointe Park. It was, however, of little consequence to my mother, who had never acknowledged Detroit's sovereignty over the back bedroom.

No matter where we lived, Pat Shine's routine was predictable. He was up before dawn every morning, shaking the furnace on cold days and filling it with coal, banging the bottom of the shovel on the lower edge of the furnace door, sending the coal flying into the fire pit where it was dispersed evenly. He told us this was something he learned when he was a railroad fireman for the Mon Con. When we complained that he awakened the entire house every morning, he told us we should at least be grateful to be waking up to a warm house.

He came home early every afternoon, read the afternoon paper, and inevitably fell asleep in his chair. After dinner we'd listen to the radio for a while, and then he went to bed, never failing to remind us that "five o'clock comes early." For people who listened to the furnace being hammered every morning at five, the reminder was unnecessary.

On Sundays, after Mass at St. Rose and when breakfast was finished, we would walk with him to Waterworks Park to stand and watch the giant wheels turning in the pumping station. It was a warm, damp place with high, arched, churchlike windows, and it always smelled of steam and oil. Sometimes we would take the small ferry across the Detroit River to Belle Isle to visit the zoo.

On the way home we would stop at McGregor's, a soda fountain at Lillibridge and Jefferson, for a malted milk or a Paddle Pop—a block of vanilla ice cream on a stick with several layers of chocolate hand-dipped by Mr. McGregor. Then we would cross Jefferson to Marty Mulligan's saloon down the block from the streetcar barns, where we would drink orange pop and eat O-Ke-Doke cheese popcorn while my father talked politics with his streetcar cronies.

He was passionate in his loyalties, to God, his family, Ireland, his adopted country, and, like every other workingman in the neighborhood, Franklin D. Roosevelt.

One Sunday morning in the autumn of 1940 I was approached as I left church by a man who said he'd pay me ten cents to deliver pamphlets to every house on Lycaste between Jefferson and Kercheval. I accepted. It was, to a ten-year-old, easy money. The man gave me the dime and a handful of "Win with Willkie" flyers promoting the candidacy of Wendell L. Willkie, a Republican who was running for president against Roosevelt.

I delivered the pamphlets, and when I got home I put the ones I had left over on the dining room table, where my father found them. He demanded to know where they had come from. I told him.

"Go and get them," he said tightly. I did.

I ran up both sides of the street collecting the flyers from the porches where I had deposited them only a short time before. One neighbor, Mr. Phelan, had already taken his inside. I knocked on his door and told him I had to have it back. He took it from the table where he had laid it and handed it back to me, asking, "Did your father send you?" I told him he had. He smiled and closed the door.

I brought the collected pamphlets to my father, and he took them—and me—to the basement and put them in the furnace. Then he asked me how much I had gotten for delivering them. A dime, I told him.

"Take it to church and put it in the poor box," he said.

The whole thing, I decided, was becoming painfully unfair, but I ran the five blocks to church, dropped the dime in the poor box, where it made a hollow sound as it hit the bottom of the empty container, and then ran home.

I sincerely believe that my dime was the only money in the poor box that day. In all the years we went to St. Rose, I can never remember seeing anyone ever put money in it. If poverty is relative, then everybody in that working-class parish probably qualified for the designation at some level. I also suspected that neither the pastor nor his assistants ever wasted time opening the box to see if, by some miracle—or mistake—someone had dropped a coin in it.

When I got home, breathless from the run, I told my father I had put the ten cents in the poor box.

"Good," he said. "That's the first thing the Republicans have ever done for poor people in this neighborhood." Then he went back to reading the Sunday paper, satisfied that he and his oldest son had done the right thing.

Thirty years later I stood on the sidewalk near St. Rose Church, long since closed, watching the wreckers pull it down. I believe that the smashed poor box, its small brass door still locked and my dime still inside, lay crushed somewhere beneath the rubble that day.

What I learned that painful Sunday was a lesson about loyalty and dedication to a principle, even though at the time it appeared to have been carried to ridiculous lengths. That my father instructed me to put my ten cents in the poor box was no surprise. My father always seemed to understand his obligation to those who had less than he, even though that obligation was narrowly defined and limited by circumstance to one small corner of southeast Detroit.

As a child I was continually confounded both by my father's philosophy of charitable giving—which to my brothers and me seemed confined largely to handing small amounts of change to people on the street who asked for it—and his personal definition of poverty. I always assumed he gave money to panhandlers because they were poor, but his characterization of who was poor and who was not was equally puzzling.

One Sunday during Mass at St. Rose we were reminded from the pulpit of a special collection for the Society of St. Vincent de Paul to aid "the poor of the parish." On our way home I asked my father who the poor of the parish were. I was looking for specifics. I wanted names.

He told me all of us were poor in some things, that some were poorer than others, and the fence that separated us was a fragile one. I was probably no older than twelve and trying to get my father to provide some understandable distinction between the poor and the nonpoor. What I needed was a straight answer, not a succession of riddles.

The panhandlers seemed to congregate on East Jefferson, near the streetcar barns at St. Jean Street and in front of Marty Mulligan's, where I suspect many of them disposed of the change they got.

Our Sunday walks were regularly delayed when these men approached my father. The scenario had a predictable sameness to it. The man would take my father a few steps away from where I was standing with my brothers, and he would talk quietly, his head down, eyes fixed on the sidewalk, while my father listened. When the talking stopped, my father would reach into his pocket, then hand the man some money, usually a nickel or a dime.

Still determined in my quest to get a reasonable definition of poorness, and conscious of my father's all-inclusive definition of the term, I would ask him if he had given the man money because he was poorer than we were. My father would reply that in some ways he was poorer than we and in other ways richer. God, he said, bestows the richness of his blessings in different ways on different people, and these men could be, despite how they looked, richer than the rich. But the most important thing of all, he said, was for us to be able to see ourselves in them.

Of course, these answers did little to add to my understanding of the social and economic differences within the neighborhood. As hard as I tried, I was unable to see myself in any of these men.

I understand now that my father had no sweeping illusions about his ability to help humanity. He helped, in a small way, the people whose circumstances had brought them to a point where they could no longer do for themselves. It was no more complicated than that. He never questioned need, never questioned motive. If people asked for help, he assumed they needed it. So he helped.

In the years since, we have come to refer to his charitable activities in those years, as humble as they were, as "Pat Shine's Unfunded Mandate." I also believe that what he represented in those years was, in its purest sense, the essence of Christian charity.

When I am out with my grandchildren, especially at sporting events, I give them money to hand to people outside the stadiums who ask us for it. When they are old enough to ask me why I do it, I will have an answer for them, one that includes at least a mention of that fragile fence.

Besides the Sunday walks, the only other regular activity involving Pat Shine and his sons was our annual safari up and down Jefferson Avenue in search of the perfect Christmas tree. Every December the vacant lots on East Jefferson were forested with hundreds of evergreens—pine, spruce, balsam, fir—and for those weeks, at least, a wonderful woodsy fragrance replaced the marshaled smells of fried foods, cigarette smoke, and stale beer expelled by the greasy exhaust fans of the bars and diners.

We usually waited until a week or so before Christmas to buy a tree, passing on our walk to Jefferson the houses of neighbors whose decorated trees blazed happily in their windows. The advantage in delaying the purchase was obvious—the closer to Christmas, the cheaper the price. The downside was that we would be dealing with trees that had been picked over for two or three weeks, with the best ones already gone.

My father believed that the Christmas-tree sellers always overbought and that even in the days before Christmas plenty of good trees were still available if a person was willing to look hard enough. The ritual involved going from one lot to another, with my father slowly walking up and down the narrow pathways between the trees, stopping every few trees to spread the boughs on one. He was looking, he always said, for a "good, stout tree." When he saw one he thought might qualify, he untied it from the wooden stake to which it had been lashed, reached through the branches, and grabbed the trunk. He lifted the tree six inches or so off the ground and then banged it sharply several times on the frozen earth.

The predictable result was a cascade of loose needles from branches that had not lived on their own for at least two months. After looking at the carpet of needles on the ground, he would lean the rejected tree against the one next to it and continue the hunt while the tree seller scowled.

With no active role in the selection process, my brothers and I stood off to the side, dragging our sleeves across running noses, stamping our feet, trying to restore circulation to toes we could no longer feel.

To Pat Shine's credit, he always managed to find a good, stout tree at the right price. But by the time the process was finished—usually two or three hours—we were too far from home to walk back, especially carrying a Christmas tree. So we took the streetcar.

Even for kids with a high embarrassment threshold, dragging a large Christmas tree on board a streetcar can tip the balance. I am convinced that the only reason we were allowed to carry something that large and unwieldy on public transportation was because my father always knew the motorman and the conductor. There was always a light exchange with them and a few chuckles about the tree before my father carried it up the narrow aisle, dragging the branches across people's laps, dislodging a few hats, and dusting riders with a light layer of pine needles. We followed, hanging back, heads down, hoping that at least some passengers might think we were not with the Christmas-tree man.

That Pat Shine worked hard for whatever we had was something that did not elude us. As he moved higher on the D.S.R. seniority list, he was able to choose his runs, and he always chose the runs that would give him the most hours. In the summer he signed on for the special runs, called trippers, to the ballpark at Michigan and Trumbull. The extra hours meant extra income.

I cannot remember his ever missing a day of work. He went to work when he was sick, saying that he wasn't sick enough to miss work. That he could collect sick pay from the city was never a factor.

In 1994, when I was undergoing radiation therapy for Hodgkin's disease and not tolerating it as well as I would have liked, my brother Bill stopped by my office one day. He told me I looked terrible. I told him I felt terrible. He asked why I had even come to work. I told him I didn't feel terrible enough to stay home.

"Blame Pa," he said.

When we were old enough to be doing our first work for pay, Pat Shine regularly preached the gospel of hard work and responsibility. He told us that if, at the end of our lives, we were remembered only for how hard we had worked, it would mean we had not wasted our lives. That was, he said, the most honest measure of success.

He told us that when we signed on to a job, the people who were paying us expected a fair return for their wage. A job, he said, did not involve seeing how much work you could avoid without getting fired but making sure you did the work you were being paid to do. Or more.

One afternoon a man got on his streetcar and breezed past the fare box without paying. "This ride's on the city," the man announced.

"The hell you say," my father responded. He signaled the motorman to stop the car and sent him to call the police while he held the passenger at bay with a switch bar, the stout iron bar used to switch tracks. He promised to brain the man if he moved.

The police came and tried to talk my father out of insisting that they write the man a ticket. They even offered to pay the six-cent fare themselves. My father told them he was doing his job and he expected them to do theirs. Reluctantly they wrote the citation. On a Saturday morning a few weeks later, his day off, my father put on a suit and tie and took a streetcar downtown to testify against the man in Traffic and Ordinance Court. The judge found the man guilty and ordered him to pay a fine of $10 or serve ten days in jail. The man paid.

My father believed that all this was simply part of his unwritten contract with the City of Detroit. In his book of D.S.R. Rules and Regulations, which was always on the dresser in his room and later found its way into the green box, rule 28 stipulates, "It is the conductor's or operator's duty to see that one fare is paid for every passenger." If that meant spending his day off seeing that the fare was paid, even after the fact, he was prepared to do that.

One summer during college I was working the 3 p.m. to 11 p.m. shift at Detroit Molding Company, an automotive supplier on Clay Avenue, when some of the workers passed the word that they were shutting down the line at 7 p.m. They said they were going to leave the plant because it was too hot to work. It was a warm night, though certainly not too hot to work, but several men had decided to go to the Tigers baseball game that night. Rather than walking out in the middle of a shift and being disciplined, or not coming to work at all that day and not being paid, they invoked the unwritten "too hot to work" option.

At seven o'clock the line stopped. Most workers punched out, including those who were not going to the ball game but were unwilling to risk the ire of the men who had instigated the walkout. The foreman said there was work for those who wanted to stay. I stayed, knowing that enduring the disfavor of my fellow workers was nothing compared with what I could expect from my father if I had to explain why I was home from work four hours early.

His workplace philosophy managed to shadow me throughout my working life. Josef Stalin died in 1953 on my day off. I was a copyboy at the *Free Press,* and I had gone to the paper to pick up my paycheck. I was leaving the city room, my check in my pocket, when an editor stopped me and told me go to the morgue and collect all the pictures of the Soviet leader. The morgue, now called the library, was a vast room filled with ranks of dark green file cabinets in which were stored a half-century's worth of clips and photographs from the pages of the newspaper. The editor, Charlie Haun, the man who had hired me three years earlier, instructed me to go through all the Stalin pictures and sort them according to the most important stages of his leadership—pre- and postrevolution, the purges, the show trials, the famine, World War II, and the Cold War.

I hurried down to the morgue. I did not for a moment consider telling him to send someone else because it was my day off. It took me about two hours to sort through the hundreds of photographs of the Soviet premier. When I brought them back to the newsroom, another editor gave me something else to do. I worked nine hours that day without being paid. By Pat Shine's standards it was simply the kind of thing that went with any job.

My brother Bill tells about the time when, still single and living at home, he came home for lunch one day when he was working as a police officer at the nearby Fifth Precinct at St. Jean and Jefferson. My father came into the kitchen from upstairs and asked him what he was doing home. Bill explained that he was on his lunch hour and that he had come home to get something to eat. Our father, retired by this time, asked him whether the criminals were also on their lunch hour. He wanted to know whether law enforcement and lawbreakers had reached some kind of cordial accommodation in which the crooks decided to suspend their felonious activities to have a quick sandwich at precisely the same time each day that the police were also lunching. "The city's not paying you to sit around eating," Pa said.

I asked Bill what he did.

"I took my sandwich and went back and ate it at the station," he said.

Both Pat and Mae were determined that their sons be properly educated. I was the first in the long and agricultural history of the Shine family to graduate from college without becoming a priest as part of the bargain. Jim also graduated from the University of Detroit and got a law degree from the Detroit College of Law. Bill got a bachelor's degree from Wayne State University and a master's from Central Michigan University. If my father had lived long enough, he would have seen the extended family add a couple of PhDs to the total. Jim worked for Chrysler's real estate division and later for ITT in New York. He retired in 2001 as senior vice president of a Boston company that operated sixty-five restaurants in New England. He worked there for thirty years.

After he left the police department, Bill worked for fourteen years as director of security for the *Free Press*. The "Favor in Hell" doctrine was not a factor. When Bill applied for the job in 1980, the paper's vice president for human resources told me, apologetically, that although Bill was a strong candidate, the *Free Press* was reluctant to hire him because I was the paper's managing editor. He said the executives wanted to avoid the appearance of favoritism.

After several weeks of interviewing other candidates for the job, the paper decided that Bill was by far the best applicant and hired him anyway. At one of the early management meetings that he attended, I complained at length about a problem in a department for which he was responsible. Don Becker, then president of the *Free Press,* turned to Bill for his response. Bill looked at me for several seconds before saying, without smiling, "I'm telling Ma."

Bill left the *Free Press* in 1994 and became director of security for the Renaissance Center, the huge downtown Detroit office complex. General Motors later moved its corporate operations there, and Bill retired in 2003 as director of security for GM's world headquarters.

I am convinced that one reason Pa encouraged us to go to college was that he believed that a person with a college education could find a job with better retirement benefits than those who had only a high school diploma. Such security was especially important to him as someone who had lived through the hard times of the Great Depression. When I told him one day in October 1950 that I had been hired by the *Free Press* as a copyboy working one day a week, he asked me only one question: "What kind of a pension plan do they have?"

Pat Shine was seventy-nine when he died. He was confined to bed the last few years of his life with arthritis so severe that he could not walk. He passed his days listening to the Tigers on the radio and talking about his life in Ireland. He never went back to the country of his birth, always telling us that "if I wanted to be in Ireland, I would have stayed there." We suspected that life on a farm in Ireland at the turn of the last century was more difficult than we might have otherwise believed and that he came to this country with few happy memories of his twenty years in Ireland. He ran away from home at least twice when he was a boy, the last time taking the family's egg money to help finance the adventure.

But he never stopped being grateful to the country that took him in and allowed him to stay with little education, no skills, and nothing more to offer than his determination to work hard and be a good citizen. His brief and standard assessment of the United States was uncomplicated. "It's a great country," he would tell us, making sure we understood what he meant.

He was proud of his military service in World War I and considered it an affirmation of his citizenship. He was proud also that his two oldest sons served their country in time of war. It was, to him, one more payment on the debt.

Whenever something good happened to one of his children—a better job, promotion, raise, honor, diploma, or degree—he responded the same way. He'd smile and nod, and we always knew what he was thinking: "It's a great country."

Let the Seller Beware

It would never occur to me to describe my mother as cheap—or even thrifty. Her view of the economic realities of the world was more complicated than that. I think she was energized simply by the challenge of confronting retailers and service providers and eventually winning. If she saved a little money along the way, it was icing on the cake.

One of her many overused axioms was "You get what you pay for," a comment she always made when something she bought at a bargain price fell apart sooner than if she had spent a little more for the better brand or nicer model. But she continued buying the cheaper stuff and, when it inevitably broke or disintegrated or stopped working, continued to remind us sadly that you get what you pay for. To this day the Shine family acknowledges the failure of any household item or appliance, regardless of its age or purchase price, by lamenting, "You get what you pay for."

She wasted nothing. She used, cleaned, and reused aluminum foil and waxed paper, throwing it away only when the sheets began to disintegrate. She left restaurants with excess saltines and oyster crackers tucked inside her purse in their cellophane packets. "What the hell," she'd say, "we paid for them." She saved rubber bands, paper clips, grocery bags, string, straight pins, and pencil stubs too short to be gripped properly. She punched her collection of thumb-tacks into small squares of corrugated paper, and no piece of clothing was ever assigned to the ragbag without first being relieved of any buttons attached thereto. In fact, no piece of clothing was ever put into one of her several ragbags until it barely met the minimum standard to qualify as a rag. She died owning enough rags to last one more lifetime.

She kept the buttons, scores of them, in a large, heavy glass jar with a decorative brass lid: shirt buttons, dress buttons, blouse buttons, suit buttons, pants buttons, coat buttons, brass buttons, fabric-covered buttons, shell buttons, mother-of-pearl buttons, fancy buttons, and plain buttons. That many of them were unique to the garments from which they had been plucked was never a consideration. They all went into the jar against the day when, as she said of all the things she saved, "They might come in handy."

They were collected in numbers that vastly outpaced their need as replacements for buttons lost by members of her family. As I have mentioned, she was not a devoted and accomplished practitioner of the homemaker's arts. She did what needed to be done and did it well enough to deflect serious criticism from outsiders. She kept a tight lid on criticism from insiders.

Whenever a button needed to be replaced, she instructed us to bring her the button jar, and she fished through it until she found a replacement close enough to the missing original to suffice. She did not expend large amounts of time digging through the button collection for an exact match. Close enough was always the prevailing standard.

I have a single and painful button memory. It involves buttons on the fly, items vital to the emotional comfort and personal well-being of young boys of that day. Losing one and not being able to avoid having it noticed by others was something much more than a minor calamity. It opened those of us unfortunate enough to experience it to the derisive cry of "Your barn door's open!" It was exponentially more humiliating if girls were within earshot and they reacted by giggling and running away.

Because of those concerns I took special care to make sure my barn door fasteners were always sewn securely in place. Whenever

I noticed even the slightest slackening in the thread, I brought the pants to my mother to have the offending button tightened. Looking back on that time, I worry now that my constant checking and rechecking of the fly area might have left the wrong impression with people who noticed it. If it did, nobody ever mentioned it, for which I am truly grateful.

The day a button pulled loose from the fly of my dark gray corduroy knickers was less traumatic than it might have been. I was eleven or twelve, and it happened late enough in the school day to make it possible for me to hurry home without its being noticed, except by those who might have thought it curious to see a kid walking quickly down the street with a religion book pressed tightly against the front of his pants.

After dinner that night I brought my pants and the button jar to my mother and asked her to replace the missing button. She did.

The next morning in school, during our first lavatory break, I stood in front of the urinal, undid one of the buttons on the fly and tried to undo the other. I could not. The button my mother had sewn in was too large for the buttonhole. It was, actually, far too large for any buttonhole, with the notable exception of the one on the garment from which it had been retrieved. How she managed to force the large button through the small hole in the first place still confounds me, but she did.

I struggled with the button as long as I could without calling attention to myself, especially from the nuns who were not reluctant to walk into the boys' lavatories to help speed things up when the process seemed to be taking too long. I knew the sisters would have found it disconcerting to see one of their charges standing at a urinal tugging frantically at the front of his pants.

The option of pulling down my pants to use one of the toilets was not an option I seriously considered. The doors of the stalls in the boys' lavatory at St. Rose had been removed, presumably to deny the protection of privacy to boys who might have been inclined to use the stalls for something other than their intended purpose. Standing with my underwear exposed to the comings and goings of my classmates—and perhaps a nun—was also not something I was prepared to do. So I wriggled in agony until dismissal time that afternoon. I would have run home, but I was reluctant to subject my bladder to any agitation. I managed to get home without incident and the second thing I did was complain to my mother about her needlework.

She took the pants and, using both hands, managed to twist the oversized button through the hole on the second or third attempt. "There," she huffed, handing me back the pants, "was that so hard?" She then declared me to be a "hopeless article" and sent me for the button jar so she could replace the button with one that actually fit the buttonhole.

I mentioned earlier that she was, by nature, suspicious of any person or any institution that might try to put something over on her. Getting swindled was a constant concern in her life, and she was determined to protect herself and her family against it. She was, she was fond of reminding us, not a dope. She knew the difference between honest merchants and those who would bilk you without blinking an eye. By her reckoning there was an alarming surplus of the latter.

As a consumer advocate she was years ahead of her time, and her sole aim seemed to be the protection of a single consumer—Mae Shine. It seemed entirely reasonable to her that she alone got to define which acts were conceived solely to take advantage of her.

Sales tax, for example.

In those years the Michigan sales tax was 3 percent. It was not a significant burden except to those who, like Mae Shine, saw it as part of a government plot to make sure the poor remained poor and the rich—well, they could damn well afford more than 3 percent.

Because of her views on the subject, her already mopey and backward kid had to deal with merchants required by law to collect the tax or he would have to deal with a mother who believed that if unfair taxation was reason enough to go to war with England, it was reason enough for her, through me, to go to war with Al of Al's Market.

Al's was typical of the independent grocery stores that were part of every Detroit neighborhood into the 1930s and 1940s. With the arrival of the supermarket in the 1950s, places like Al's were destined to become part of urban history, alive only in our memories.

At stores like Al's the prices were fair, the selection limited but adequate, and the service friendly. Most would extend credit to their regular customers, an uncomplicated process that involved telling whoever was behind the counter, "My mother says to please put it on her bill." No carrying charges, no late fees; you could pay a little something on the tab when you had the money. If you really needed something but were unable to get to the store, most store owners were happy to send one of their children to the house with your order, even if it was only a quart of milk or a loaf of bread.

Perhaps the most appealing feature of those stores was that one was always a few steps from your house, no matter where you lived. Al's was on Lycaste near Jefferson, about three doors from our house, so it was our store of choice for staples. Since home refrigeration involved a heavy wooden icebox containing a twenty-five-pound block of ice and not a lot of room for things that needed to be kept cold, grocery shopping was a daily activity.

It was impossible to walk more than a block in that neighborhood—or in any other Detroit neighborhood—without coming across a small, family-run grocery store. Within blocks of our house, in addition to Al's, were stores run by the Bakalises, Gabriels, Bogoses, Kanes, Mowids, Iubes, Zogbys, and Burgoynes. The Jefferson Quality Market was run by the Pinkertons, and James's Market on Jefferson near St. Jean was owned by Jimmy Shaib, who always called my friend Peachy "Beachy."

John Markus had a store at the opposite end of our block at Lycaste and Kercheval. My longtime friend the late Nick Krust, who became a Thirty-sixth District Court judge in Detroit, was John Markus's nephew and came most summer days from his parents' house in Highland Park to help his uncle and cousins at the market. It was his earliest experience in pro bono work. He often told us how he marveled at the resourcefulness of John Markus, and the others like him, to be able to achieve even marginal success in marginal businesses in marginal neighborhoods.

Nick's favorite story of those days involved the time his Uncle John sent him to the Detroit Bank and Trust branch on Hillger and Jefferson, two blocks from the store, to get change for a five-dollar bill. Nick hurried to the bank, gave the teller the money, and asked that it be changed into nickels, dimes, and quarters. The teller looked at the bill and then took it to the office of the manager, who returned with the bill in hand to ask Nick where he got it. Nick told him. The manager said the bill was counterfeit and that the bank was going to have to keep it. Nick started to cry, having a good idea of what awaited him if he went back to the store without either the five dollars or the equivalent in change. It was an amount that probably represented a serious percentage of that week's net profit.

The manager let him call Uncle John, who arrived at the bank minutes later in his white apron and out of breath. The manager explained the situation and asked Uncle John if he remembered who gave it to him. He said he did not. The manager said he had to turn the bill over to the government and that he was sorry, but Mr. Markus would not be reimbursed for his loss.

Uncle John then told the manager that he did, indeed, remember who had given him the bad bill. He asked the manager to give him back the five dollars and said he would take care of the matter himself. No need, he said, to involve the federal government in a matter that could just as easily be handled at a local level. The manager said he was sorry, but he could not return the bill. The law required him to turn it in.

According to Nick, Uncle John then launched into a long, plaintive, and personal recitation of the vicissitudes of the immigrant experience. Nick said he had heard it before. He called it Uncle John's "Huddled Masses" speech. Aproned and eloquent, John Markus explained in painful detail his decision to leave home and family in Greece and travel as a young man to this glorious land of opportunity. Although he had no friends here and was unable to speak the language, he was motivated by his dream of a better life for himself and for his children in this golden place called America. He came with no money, little education, and no skills. All he had to offer, he said, was a determination to succeed and the resolve to be a good American.

He told of how he had come to Detroit, to this bank, to this very manager, where he had gotten a loan to open his small store. He had worked hard, seven long days a week, month after month, repaid the loan without ever missing a payment, without ever being late, and, most important, without ever asking for any special consideration. He was an American citizen and wanted to be treated no better, but certainly no worse, than any of his fellow Americans. So he asked for no favors.

And now he stood before his friend the banker asking for a small favor, one involving five dollars, so he could remedy an unfortunate situation in his own way, only to be turned away as if he were a stranger. It was not, he said sadly, what he had come to expect of America.

The speech had its desired effect. The manager wavered. He handed Uncle John the five-dollar bill, making him vow to never, ever tell anybody about what had happened. He said he expected Uncle John to resolve the matter discreetly and wanted to hear no more about it. And he certainly did not ever want to see that five-dollar bill again.

Nick remembered walking back to the store that day with his uncle, who kept turning the bill over in his hands, looking at it first with his glasses and then without them, pronouncing it as authentic-looking as any five-dollar bill he had ever seen. But money was the banker's business, he told his nephew, and if he said it was a fake, then it was a fake.

Nick asked him who had given him the bill.

"How the hell do I know?"

"What are you going to do with it?" Nick asked.

"Give it to the milkman," he replied.

The next morning Nick watched as the driver from Twin Pines Farm Dairy brought in the milk order and Uncle John counted out the money to pay him, including the questionable five, and gave it to the milkman.

Later that day, Nick said, his uncle took him aside, put his arm over his shoulder, and told him quietly: "Look, kid, Twin Pines is a big company. They have a lot of money. I am a poor man. I work hard every day and I still don't have a lot of money. If they have to give that five dollars back to the government, it's not going hurt them as much as it would have hurt me."

Talking about it fifty years later, Nick and our friend Jim Pikulas, whose business experience dated from his childhood in his father's small diner on Grand River, decided that it was a reasonable economic policy and one that made sense for that time, in those circumstances, and certainly in that neighborhood.

But I was going to tell you about my life as a reluctant tax protester. It involved our daily purchase from Al's Market of one quart of milk and one loaf of bread. Milk was fifteen cents for a one-quart carton, and bread was ten cents a loaf. When my mother sent me for those items, she gave me twenty-five cents, even though she knew that, with a one-cent tax, the total due Al was twenty-six cents.

Rather than burden Al with my mother's views on the basic unfairness of a tax structure that added a penny to the cost of bread and milk, the basic foods required to keep a family fed and healthy, I devised my own plan to stiff the state for the penny I did not have. I did it not to further my mother's antitax agenda but to save me from the embarrassment of having to confront Al every night over a penny.

What I did instead was buy the milk, give Al the quarter, and leave with the milk and my ten cents in change. When I got outside I would turn around, pretend I had forgotten the bread, pick up a loaf, and hand him the dime.

One day after I had been doing my doorway pirouette for a few weeks, I came back for the bread. Al was standing behind the counter holding a loaf of Bond Bread in his hand. He said something like, "Listen, sonny, we don't have to go through this every night.

Just take the bread and milk, and give me the quarter. The tax man can manage without the penny."

I could feel my face burning. My humiliation was complete. Every afternoon from that day on, I took the bread and milk, sheepishly handed him the quarter, and left, still too embarrassed to say anything to him except "Thank you."

When someone to whom I told this story asked why I didn't just toss in a penny of my own each time, I had to explain that, given the extent of my disposable income in those years, I did not walk around with a pocketful of pennies in case I needed one whenever my mother balked at paying her legal share of the sales tax. Remember, pennies had purchasing power in those days.

Although my mother seemed to get along well with all the neighborhood merchants, they understood that when it came to dealing with Mrs. Shine, the overriding factor in the transaction was always going to be economic, friendship notwithstanding.

If the philosophy of caveat emptor was embraced by prudent shoppers, her approach was more along the lines of caveat vendor. Consequently, my trips to the store also meant return trips to the same store to return groceries that did not meet her standards, which were always significantly higher than those set by the U.S. Food and Drug Administration or the State Department of Health.

I was sent back with cans that were dented; fruit that was bruised; slightly wilted lettuce; soft tomatoes; bananas mottled with brown spots; flaccid celery; mushy green peppers; meat, especially hamburger, that was sticky to the touch; eggs that were too small or carried the remnants of henhouse residue; lunch meat sliced too thick or too thin; hot dogs with traces of color not natural to the original product; milk she decided was turning sour, or "curdled," as she called it. She could tell, or said she could tell, when a head of cabbage or a rutabaga had been dropped and sent those back as well.

If there was a small positive in any of this, it was that since childhood my mother had no sense of smell, the result of a severe case of influenza during the worldwide epidemic near the end of

World War I. When she decided something looked bad—"tainted," she called it—she was sure it probably smelled bad as well. So she would stick the offending product under my nose and order me to smell it. Willing to do anything to avoid another painful trip back to the store, my answer was always the same: "Smells okay to me." She did not have an elevated trust level and simply assumed I was lying, and she'd send it back despite my assurances.

Whenever store employees saw me walking into their store carrying a bag, their expression did not encourage me in my mission. Although they never asked, "What in God's name is your mother unhappy with now?" I knew that's what they were thinking. My opening line was standard: "My mother says this is—" Then I filled in the specific complaint of stale, tainted, spotted, bruised, limp, rancid, old, moldy, curdled, sticky, dented, too thick, too thin, doesn't look right or smells funny, something of which she had no personal olfactory knowledge but that she strongly suspected, which was always good enough for her.

Befitting my status as mope, whenever I had to return things, I lurked outside the store until any customers inside had left. It was torture enough being mortified in front of the store owner and the employees without allowing strangers to participate in my discomfort.

If only she had been so particular about the fit of our clothes. Buying clothes or shoes for us was an uncomplicated process. She never bought anything that fit. Why spend good money, she reasoned, for something that will be too small in a year? Better to buy something that will be just right in a year, even though your kids, in the meantime, will all look like refugees dressed in clothes salvaged from a surplus bin.

We bought our shoes mostly at a Buster Brown shoe store on Jefferson called Campbell's. The sales staff was trained to measure feet and sell shoes that fit. My mother's exchanges with them were predictable.

My mother (squeezing the new oxford on my foot and pinching it to find my big toe): "They're too small."

The salesman: "It's his size."

My mother: "I told you they were too small."

The salesman: "They'll stretch."

My mother: "You'll stretch. Get him the next size."

I always left the store with my feet swimming in shoes that were too large, but I was confident in the belief that in a year or so they'd start getting comfortable.

My brother Bill still insists that his recurring foot problems are a direct result of a pair of buckle shoes she bought for him at Thom McAn's shoe store. Bill claims they never fit right and that she made him keep them because they were on sale, a charge my mother denied every time the matter was raised, which was often.

My earliest recollection of my mother's confronting Detroit's retail giants dates to sometime in the late 1930s. We lived in the rented house on Beniteau, not far from the river. We had lived in a furnished house, and the move to Beniteau required a substantial purchase of new furniture. So my mother and father went downtown to Crowley's department store and bought everything we needed—from the kitchen to the dining room to the living room and the bedrooms. Because it is the American way, they bought it on credit.

It wasn't long before they fell behind on the payments. The city had reduced my father's workweek to four days, and a family that had been barely making it on full pay was now trying to get by with 20 percent less.

One morning, while my father was at work, a Crowley's truck pulled up in front of our house. Two men—a driver and his younger helper—knocked on our door and said they had come to pick up the furniture. Standing next to them was a court bailiff holding a clipboard with the writ of replevin, a court order allowing Crowley's to repossess our furniture. The writ also listed the items to be recovered, which was virtually everything in the house.

My brother Jim and I watched from behind the screen door. I was about seven, Jim five. Bill, about two at the time, was in a playpen in the living room.

Mae Shine stood on the porch, hands on her hips, and planted herself squarely in front of our door while the driver, who was not demonstrating an abundance of enthusiasm for the task at hand, explained quietly to her why they were there.

The bailiff, on the other hand, was a self-important functionary with a large stomach who seemed overly impressed with his role. He wore an old gray fedora, a white shirt and a dark tie, and wide black suspenders. He kept interrupting the driver, shaking his clipboard, and reminding my mother that he had a court order empowering Crowley's to remove any furniture or appliances listed thereon.

My mother ignored him and concentrated on the driver, who seemed like a nice person; my mother undoubtedly had already identified him as a reasonably decent man and therefore the most vulnerable player in this little drama. She could see that he was clearly not as excited about his part in the unhappy task as the bailiff seemed to be. The helper stood to one side, uninvolved. His job was to carry things, and he was apparently waiting to be given the order to lift something.

My mother continued to argue with the driver. She explained to him that my father was a longtime City of Detroit employee and, like all the streetcar men at the time, was working fewer hours. She pointed out that we were only a few months in arrears, and it was only a question of time before we became current with our payments. All we needed was a little time.

The driver told her that was between her and Crowley's credit department, that he was only doing his job, which was to pick up the furniture listed on the writ and take it back to the warehouse. She would be doing the right thing, he said awkwardly, if she stepped aside and let him do his job. He explained encouragingly that we could probably get it all back as soon as we brought our indebtedness to a level that Crowley's was comfortable with. It would all work out in the end, he assured her.

My mother believed none of it. She knew instinctively that if the furniture ever left the house, it was never coming back. It was also clear to us from the start, even as young as we were, that the furniture was going nowhere. Stepping aside was not part of Mae Shine's genetic makeup. We had never seen her do it before and did not expect it to happen on this occasion, especially since she was operating on home ground.

She continued to work on the driver. We had a good credit record, she told him, and always paid our bills. We were good citizens and not deadbeats. My father had worked for the city for more than twenty years and had been a soldier in the war. She said she had a hard time understanding Crowley's rush to take her furniture after only a few missed payments. She suggested he come back when her husband was home and speak with him. He said he could not come back, that he had been ordered to pick up the furniture that day. The bailiff again tried to interrupt, tapping the court order on the clipboard with his pencil. My mother told him to mind his own business, that this was between her and the driver, whose defenses, she sensed, were beginning to crumble.

They were about thirty minutes into the discussion when it became obvious that she was running out of arguments as well as time. The driver had taken off his cap by this time and was almost pleading with her to let him take the furniture. The helper, hands deep in his pockets, was leaning against the porch post, obviously bored by the whole thing. The bailiff raised his clipboard again and started moving toward my mother as he repeated what he had said earlier about the court order. She shot him a look, a clear warning that if he messed with her, he would be messing with the wrong woman. She took a half step in his direction. He took a full step back and shut up.

Finally, my mother played her last card. She stepped away from the screen door and pulled it open.

"Take it," she said with a sweeping wave of her hand. "Take it all." She told him we had paid too much for it in the first place, that it was junk, and that she could get better furniture for what we still owed on it.

The driver walked toward the door, his helper, suddenly alert, close behind. The bailiff stayed put, ready to check off each item on his clipboard as it was loaded on the truck.

The driver had one foot inside the house when my mother pointed at my brothers and me and told him: "And while you're at it take them, too. If you're going to take their beds, you might as well take them, too."

Take them to Mr. Crowley's house, she said, and let them sleep in one of his bedrooms.

For my brothers and me it was not one of childhood's golden moments. Not only had people come to take our furniture, now our mother was giving us to a truck driver from Crowley's.

The driver froze. He looked at us and saw two bewildered kids and an infant, the older two looking like they were about to cry as they waited to see if he was going to take them away. Then he turned and quickly left the house.

"To hell with it," he said. "We're not taking this furniture." He went back to his truck, his young helper hurrying after him. The bailiff shook his clipboard a couple more times in my mother's direction but said nothing and did not linger on the porch. He hurried to his car and drove off after the truck.

My father and mother were able to work out a repayment program, and they got to keep the furniture—and the kids. More than sixty years later most of the furniture she described as junk is still in the family: sturdy oak pieces, as substantial as and looking as good as—or better than—they did all those years ago when Crowley's efforts to reclaim them failed miserably on the front porch of 635 Beniteau.

I mentioned earlier how unhappy my mother was when I wrote about this incident in 1985 in the *Free Press*. Besides threatening to sue me for slander and invasion of her privacy, she said she was afraid to open her newspaper every morning, worried about what personal family secrets I had decided to share with several hundred thousand other people.

Of the Crowley's column, she said, "Now everybody thinks I'm a deadbeat."

When I reminded her that it had all happened nearly fifty years earlier, she was not placated. She said that people believed that once a deadbeat, always a deadbeat. Which was, in fact, simply an extension of her own philosophy, that a leopard does not change its spots and that things like being a deadbeat have no statute of limitations.

Mae Shine's run-ins with those who represented a challenge to her sense of self-worth or a threat to her economic well-being were not always spontaneous. Sometimes, she planned ahead.

When she decided to visit Ireland in 1949 with my youngest brother, Bill, her first trip back since 1927, she bought their tickets a year early. Again, the decision was made not out of efficiency but for economic reasons. In 1948 Bill was twelve, and children twelve and under traveled at half fare, an economic benefit that would not have been possible if she had waited until the next year to buy his ticket.

Bill was tall for his age, and every time they strolled the deck of the Cunard liner *Britannic*, he recalls, my mother kept reminding him under her breath not to stand so straight. Ship's officers were everywhere, and she worried that one would spot her with her lanky son and wonder why he was traveling at a cut-rate fare.

Bill remembers that she admonished him about his posture so many times on that trip that he adopted a permanent slouch and walked around bent in half even when he was by himself.

"We shared a table in the dining room with some nice old ladies, and they kept looking at me with these sad expressions," Bill said. "I could just imagine them saying to each other, 'He's such a well-mannered boy and she dresses him so nicely. It's a pity he's so deformed.' I think they thought we were on our way to Lourdes to see if the Blessed Virgin could do something about my condition."

Ma's instructions to us about standing too straight defied the universal maternal instruction about posture. While mothers the world over were ordering their kids to stand straight, she was always telling us not to—on streetcars and buses; on the Detroit and Cleveland Navigation Company's steamers to Cleveland, where we would get on the train to Pittsburgh; on the train to Pittsburgh.

My mother believed that being required to pay full fare for her children on any conveyance was a capitalist plot to impoverish her and further enrich the transportation moguls. So she didn't. She never bothered to explain how she reconciled this theory with her aversion to paying any fare at all for her children on buses and streetcars owned and operated by the city.

For the most part, getting away without paying her children's fare presented little challenge. Every Department of Street Railways streetcar or bus had a raised marker on the pole next to the fare box. It measured forty-four inches from the floor. People who were taller than forty-four inches paid, people shorter than forty-four inches did not.

She always ushered us quickly past the fare box, each of us in our Hunchback of Notre Dame posture, as she dropped in fare only for herself. Sometimes the streetcar conductor or bus driver would look at the three junior Quasimodos scuttling quickly down the aisle and then look at my mother as if he might say at any minute, "You gonna pay for those kids?" But she'd stare right back, and the driver/conductor would let it go, probably deciding that he'd already had a bad enough day without antagonizing a woman who looked as if she was spoiling for a fight.

I think she believed this might go on forever. But one Sunday she was confronted by the driver of a bus who seemed to be made of sterner stuff than most of his wishy-washy colleagues.

We had been downtown, and when we got on the Jefferson bus to go home, my brothers and I hurried, as usual, past the fare box and crab-walked down the aisle, staying as close to the floor of the bus as possible. When it became clear to the driver that my mother was counting out six cents to pay for her fare, while we hurried toward the back of the bus, he told her: "You gotta pay for those kids too, lady."

In a voice that made it clear that she was highly offended, maybe even insulted, she replied: "I certainly do not have to pay for them. They're only children."

The driver told her she had to pay for her children if they were taller than the marker. He told her to bring us back to the front of the bus and have us stand next to the marker. If we were shorter than the forty-four inches, she would not have to pay for us—and they both knew that we were all taller than the marker.

"I absolutely will not bring them up here and subject them to your humiliating little test," she said. When she saw us squirming nervously, she glared at us, one of her patented looks that pinned us to the seat.

"Then put eighteen cents in the fare box for them," the driver said. She told him she was not going to do that, either. She then launched what has to have been the most brilliant and effective filibuster ever conducted on public transportation in America.

She talked about fairness and equity, about commonsense enforcement of rules, about government's responsibilities to its citizens, and about the God-given right of all Americans to travel freely without being bullied by tyrannical agents of a transit system whose executives would be appalled to witness this sad spectacle of a rider and her family being publicly abused and humiliated in the city's name, and all for eighteen cents, for God's sake.

By this time the other riders on the bus had stopped reading their newspapers or talking with their friends and turned their attention to the urban drama unfolding at the front of the bus. Jim, Bill, and I were properly impressed with, and maybe even proud of, Mae Shine's performance. The bus stopped and started. People got on and off, although I think some passengers may have ridden past their stops, curious to see how all this was going to play out. My mother kept talking.

Whenever she paused, the driver said: "Eighteen cents, lady."

She talked about there being no price tag on principle, and, if there was, it certainly wasn't eighteen cents. She said she was the wife of a city employee and that all tax-paying Detroiters, not just families of city workers, deserved better treatment than this at the hands of the people being paid to serve them.

The driver, unmoved, repeated his demand for eighteen cents.

Finally, my mother said to him: "I am tired of arguing with you. Why don't you just stop and let us off?"

He wheeled the bus to the curb at the next corner, happy at the prospect of finally being rid of his troublesome passenger and her freeloading children.

The bus stopped, the doors rattled open, and we scrambled off behind our mother. She smiled gloriously as she watched the bus drive off.

It was our stop.

What made her triumph even sweeter was that the driver, intent on collecting fares for her children, had failed to notice that she had neglected to drop in her own fare.

The truth of the matter is, she was used to winning. I cannot remember a confrontation with a merchant or a retailer—at any level—in which my mother was ever bested. Back then, profit margins were frighteningly narrow and the concept that the customer is always right did not enjoy wide acceptance in the local business community. As a result store owners, managers, clerks, and salespeople actively resisted refunds, credits, or exchanges, all of which they saw as a serious threat to profitability.

So when they encountered people like my mother, they were determined to resist their demands. But my mother never went into battle unprepared, because she knew her opponents would not go down without a struggle and almost certainly not after the first salvo. But, sooner or later, they all went down, even the J. L. Hudson department store.

In 1950, after more than a year of longing for them, I got a pair of gray flannel slacks for my birthday. They were, along with white buckskin shoes—which I did not have—the ultimate fashion symbol for the well-dressed college man at the University of Detroit.

Gray flannel slacks were the uniform of choice for the Grosse Pointe kids, most of whom I regarded with a passionate envy, especially when they breezed past me in their nice cars every day after school as I waited on West McNichols for the bus.

Although it is true that I was technically one of them—our

house on Wayburn had a Grosse Pointe Park address, and I slept in a bedroom in the Grosse Pointe part of the house—Wayburn, as I mentioned earlier, was in the part of the city called the Cabbage Patch. This set us apart from the people who lived in the bigger, nicer houses on the streets farther east and whose kids had their own cars and wore gray flannel slacks and white bucks to school. But our location was also a badge my mother wore proudly.

My new pants were as soft as a mouse's ear. I loved them. I wore them to school every day for more than a year and on most weekends as well. One day I felt a disturbing draft and realized my wonderful trousers were wearing out—in the crotch. I continued wearing them until it was clear that I was getting dangerously close to violating U of D's dictum about modest clothing and the city's ordinances relating to indecent exposure.

So one morning, with more than a little sadness, I rolled them up and dropped them on the floor of my closet. A few days later my mother walked into the kitchen while I was having breakfast. She had the gray flannels in her hand. She wanted to know why I had rolled them in a ball and tossed them on the floor of my closet.

"They're worn out," I said.

"Worn out?" she repeated. "These are brand new."

It was her standard response to any situation in which something in our house, regardless of age or frequency of use, broke, failed, or wore out before she thought it should. Her own extravagant expectations, I should add, outdistanced even the most generous warranties.

"They're nearly two years old," I told her and showed her the tattered crotch, which she regarded with awe.

"This is a disgrace," she said. "I'm taking these back."

That she would return the pants and get her money back was a given. It would never have occurred to me—or to anyone else who knew her well—to consider any other outcome.

Later that week she put the gray flannels in an old shopping bag, got on a bus, and took them downtown to the J. L. Hudson Company, where she had bought them.

My recollection of the second-floor men's department at Hudson's is that it was somber and intimidating, a place with dark, wood-paneled walls, subtle lighting, thick carpets, alcoves with three-way mirrors, and fitting rooms with narrow, louvered doors that ended two feet short of the floor. There were endless racks of expensive suits, brands like Hart, Schaffner & Marx, and Hickey-Freeman, and salesmen who moved quietly through the department, waiting on customers or fussing endlessly with the suits, mostly blues and grays, arranging and rearranging them on the racks. The salesmen were always as well dressed as their customers, and it was often hard to tell them apart. And it was always quiet.

Years later I found it difficult to imagine what the reaction must have been the morning my mother strode purposefully off the escalator and into those pretentious surroundings, my worn-out gray flannels in her shopping bag.

She told us she walked up to the first salesman she saw, pulled the pants from the shopping bag, and told him they had worn out and that she wanted her money back. She said he took the pants from her, held them gingerly with his thumb and forefinger as if they might be contaminated by a deadly strain of some fabric-borne pathogen, and dropped them on a desk. He then examined the back of the cuffs on the inside and announced smugly that the material of the pants had been rubbed nearly threadbare by the backs of the shoes, a clear indication of excessive wear. The pants, he said, had simply worn out from excessive use. There would be no refund.

My mother argued that these were expensive pants, a quality brand, purchased in good faith at Detroit's top store, and they absolutely should not have disintegrated simply because they were worn "excessively." She noted the absence of any label on the pants warning the consumer that "excessive wear" could result in their falling apart before their time. He ignored her when she asked him for the official Hudson definition of "excessive wear."

The salesman, whom she described as a "stuffy old gobshite," was unmoved by her arguments. The owner of the pants, he said, had simply worn them out, the fate of any piece of apparel, regardless of quality, that is misused. There would be no refund. He handed the pants back to her.

She told us later that seven or eight customers were in the department being fitted for suits at the time. They stood in front of the mirrors while solicitous salesmen tugged and pulled at the sleeves and tails of the suit jackets and ran their hands across the shoulders.

Ever the populist, Mae Shine decided to take her case directly to the people. She turned to the other customers, held the flannels in one hand, and thrust the other through the ragged remnants of the crotch. She turned slowly to make sure they had all seen it, before inquiring loudly: "I ask you, as reasonable people, is this what the J. L. Hudson Company considers quality merchandise? Is this the kind of workmanship we can look forward to from now on when we buy our clothes here?"

She made one more slow turn, her hand still poking through the frayed strips of flannel, making sure each customer got another good look at the pants.

Before a vote could be taken, the salesman grabbed the pants from my mother's upraised hands and threw them in a wastebasket next to the desk. Then he went into the back room to fill out a slip crediting her charge for the full amount of the purchase.

When I got home from school that afternoon, the credit slip was proudly displayed on the dining room table. Next to it were the crotchless gray flannels. While the "gobshite" was in back doing the paperwork, she had taken the pants out of the wastebasket and put them back in her shopping bag. I asked her why, in God's name, she had brought them home.

"What the hell," she said. "I can fix these."

A few days later she cut a swatch of heavy gray fabric from a discarded gabardine overcoat and used it to replace the worn-out crotch.

The pants, sadly, were never the same. I wore them once to school, and by the end of the day the inside of my thighs had been rubbed red by the rough gabardine patches. This forced me to walk in an unnatural way to reduce the friction, something that attracted considerable attention.

About a month later, perhaps emboldened by her earlier success, she went back to Hudson's with a gray wool shirt, a Pendleton that belonged to brother Bill. His affinity for the shirt was such that he, like me, wore it to school virtually every day. It wore out in the elbows. She got her money back without a major confrontation, brought the shirt home, and repaired it with patches cut from the shirt's tail, allowing Bill to get a couple more years of wear.

I'm sure a therapist could trace my aversion to solo shopping of virtually any kind straight back to my traumatic childhood marketplace experiences with my mother. In fact, my case would probably qualify as a perfect in-basket exercise at a meeting of the American Psychological Association.

Phyllis buys all my clothes—shoes, shirts, suits, ties, socks, underwear, handkerchiefs—and her sense of fashion is unerring. Whenever I shop for gifts for her, I recruit an adviser from among my daughters. I avoid grocery stores except when necessity dictates otherwise. When I do shop and put the groceries on the kitchen counter, I can hear my mother's voice: "Did you even look at these bananas before you bought them? Take them back and get some that don't look like they were picked last month!" And that pales next to my fear that a salesperson will see my name on a credit card and ask: "Didn't your mother used to shop here?"

Mae and her sons (*from left*) Neal, Jim, and Bill,
behind the Shine house at 635 Beniteau, 1937.

Mae (*left*) with Aunt Mary
(*center*) and Aunt Kate,
in Pittsburgh with Neal (*left*)
and Jim, 1934.

Mae with her sister Kitty
in the back garden of their
house the day Mae left
Ireland, 1927.

Pat Shine, the conductor, ready for work, ca. 1930.

Mary Ellen Conlon Shine, ca. 1970.

Neal and Jim in the backyard of the Shine house, 635 Beniteau,
on a Monday, with Mrs. Fries's wash already on the line, 1934.

Annie Conlon behind the Conlon house at Kingston Terrace,
Carrick-on-Shannon, with one of the Gorman children, 1954.

Neal Shine with his grandparents in front of 4 Kingston Terrace, 1954.

Tommy "the Glazier" McDermott hauling Neal's suitcase
to the railroad station, with James Conlon walking alongside, 1954.

Phyllis Theresa Knowles, the adorable tenth-grader, 1947.

Spiritual Bouquet

✠

Masses 5

Holy Communion 7

Rosaries 4

Ejaculations 1

Way of the cross 3

Visits to the Blessed Sacrament 7

May the Mother of Christ
From her high throne above
Shower blessings this day
On the Mother I love.

*Neal and Jim
on Mothers day
May 12 1940*

The legendary Mother's Day Spiritual Bouquet card, 1940.

Left to right: Jim, Neal, and Bill in front of 4 Kingston Terrace,
Carrick-on-Shannon, with Mae's ashes, 1990.

Mae Shine (*right*), with her neighbor Patsy Mann, "the belle of Belfast City," dancing a jig at the wedding of her grandson Jim, 1982.

Pat and Mae Shine in Pat's Victory Garden at the Shine house, 1532 Lycaste, 1944.

James and Bridget Conlon next to 4 Kingston Terrace, 1954.

Quality People

My mother was acutely conscious of status. I think it was probably a condition of the culture in which she was raised. She believed that some people were to the manor born and then there were the rest of us. She was convinced that no matter how well you did in life, it was not possible to elevate your social status. It all came down to the accident of birth.

It was not that she believed that those born to wealth and privilege were necessarily any better than we were. It was just that we would never be like them, any more than they would ever be like us. It was less a question of money than it was of station. She never stood in awe of those she called "the quality." She simply recognized it as reality and came to terms with it.

She dismissed our arguments that her thinking was rooted deep in the colonialism of old Ireland. We told her that in America people could be whatever their dreams and aspirations told them they could be, and they could exist at whatever social level they could manage. This was not the Ireland of her childhood, which was run by the English, we said.

Maybe not, she said, but hadn't we in this country been so enamored of England's nobility that we created an aristocracy of our own? Had not Detroit's auto magnates and merchants built for themselves noble dwellings and manor houses in the style of the English, given them English names like Cloverleigh, Stonehurst,

Rose Terrace, Edgemere, and Drybrook? That most of the streets in Grosse Pointe Park—streets like Bedford, Berkshire, Buckingham, Middlesex, Hampton, Balfour, Nottingham, Kensington, Devonshire, Somerset, Yorkshire, and even Wayburn—were named for English places wasn't just happenstance, she said.

She did acknowledge, however, that more things were possible for her children and grandchildren in America than she ever dared dream of in Ireland. In a letter to her sister Gertie in 1958, she included news about my brother Jim and his fiancée, Barbara Unti, now his wife: "Jim and Barbara both graduate from U.D. this week. I'd be a long time in Carrick before I could see my boys graduate from college. This sure is God's country, every one is as good as the next."

But even as she reminded us to always be proud of our accomplishments, of the good things we had done with our lives, of how far we had come from Kerry's picturesque hills and Carrick-on-Shannon's quiet lanes, part of her, I'm convinced, still believed that we had our place and "the quality" had theirs and there was no real chance that the twain would ever meet.

That she felt that way did not surprise us. She had been a servant in Ireland when she was fourteen, working for a doctor in one of the fine houses in St. George's Terrace, the part of Carrick-on-Shannon where the "quality" people lived.

The caste system was sharply defined, by religion and ancestry. Most people who lived in St. George's Terrace were Protestants of English or Scottish origin and were the leading merchants, landlords, and professionals. She understood that she lived in one world and that they lived in another. It was, she said, something that everybody in Carrick understood and accepted.

She knew that she could read the social notes in the Leitrim newspaper without ever seeing her name or the names of her friends.

"A musical entertainment was held in the Town Hall, Carrick-on-Shannon, on last Friday night, and was attended with great success. There was a large and fashionable attendance, many of the *elite* of the counties of Roscommon and Leitrim being present."

It was always a safe conclusion that the list of the elite and fashionable would not include any of the Conlons—or the McGreevys, Doyles, Morans, Grahams, Dolans, McDermotts, Flynns, Costellos, Mulherns, Cassidys . . .

The first day of our two-week stay in 1984 at Glin Castle, the place my mother called "the symbol of everything that was ever wrong" with Ireland, remains strong in my memory.

I am sure she was overwhelmed at the sight of this two-hundred-year-old house, a gleaming Gothic presence overlooking the Shannon River. My mother was strangely silent as we got out of the car and walked to the front door. When we got to the door she hesitated, ushering the rest of us before her into the entry hall before stepping slowly across the threshold.

I still think about what must have been going through her mind at that moment. She was back in Ireland again but not in the Ireland she remembered; this was Ireland of the big houses, the grand demesnes, places where the likes of country girls from Leitrim did not saunter through the front door big as life, acting as if they belonged. She was clearly uncomfortable.

The next morning at breakfast I reminded her that we had rented the place, and it was, for two weeks, effectively our home. I suggested, lightly, that we should all try to act, at least for the remainder of our stay, as if we belonged.

She turned to me, her face set, and said, without smiling: "I know where I belong, and I know where you belong, and it's not in a place like this." Then she left the room and went back to her new friends in the kitchen. Despite whatever misgivings she might have had, she settled in quickly. In the evenings, while the rest of us chatted and sipped Bailey's Irish Cream in front of a fire in one of the castle's elegant drawing rooms, my mother more often than not was down in the scullery with the women who worked at the castle, Nancy Ellis; her sister, Mai Liston; and Una Bourke. They talked late into the evening, the sound of their laughter making us wonder if they might not be having a better time than we were.

Ma's favorite among these women who cooked for us and looked after our needs during those two wonderful weeks seemed to be Nancy Ellis. She was eleven years younger than my mother and had come to work in the kitchen at Glin Castle when she was sixteen. Her great-grandfather had been the gamekeeper at the castle, and her grandfather had been the Knight of Glin's coachman. Nancy had never married and, despite my mother's promise to find her a wealthy husband if she came to America, she worked for the Knight of Glin at the castle until she retired in 1993. She died ten years later. Her niece carried on the family tradition at Glin Castle.

Mae Shine was clearly more comfortable with her new friends in the kitchen than she was in the other parts of the castle, where she seemed to make a special effort to walk softly, especially on the grand staircase in the entrance hall, as if someone might stop her and ask what she was doing there.

Although she never said as much, I think she may have seen in Nancy Ellis a mirror image of her own life if she had stayed in Ireland. Regardless of how cordial and gracious Desmond FitzGerald, the Knight of Glin, was, and how much he and his wife, Olda, were admired and respected by the people who worked for them, having a job like Nancy's was not what my mother had in mind for her life. It was, in fact, the reason she left Ireland.

Seamus, my mother's youngest brother, remembers that their father, James, spent a lot of time tipping his hat. "I wouldn't say my father was servile or anything," Seamus said, "but it seems he tipped his hat to everybody in Carrick above the rank of Jim McLoughlin, the street sweeper."

My mother's abiding concern was that any success her children enjoyed would turn their heads. Every career advancement was met with her warning not to "get too full of yourself." Every honor or award prompted her to caution: "There's more plaques in the world than people, and sooner or later everyone gets one." She worried that we would forget our origins, forget whence we had sprung, and forget the forebears who made everything in our lives possible. She had no patience with people who saw their accomplishments as personal triumphs, giving no credit to the people in their lives who made the success possible. She also believed deeply that behind every honor and achievement in life lurked the very real possibility of failure, something she called a comedown. It was a circumstance she believed we all needed to seriously consider and be prepared for.

Every time I got a promotion at the *Free Press,* her congratulations were tempered with the same warning: "Don't ever forget that you're a jumped-up copyboy, and you can go down as fast as you came up."

I retired from the *Free Press* in the summer of 1989 when I was senior managing editor and a three-days-a-week columnist. Nine months later, while I was vacationing in Miami with my wife and daughter Peggy, I got a call from the late Jim Batten, the chairman of the board of Knight Ridder, then the parent company of the *Free Press,* asking me to meet with him at the company's Miami headquarters. I met with Batten, along with Tony Ridder, then president of KR's newspaper division and later the KR board chairman, and Jennie Buckner, then corporate vice president for news and who retired in 2004 as executive editor of the *Charlotte Observer.* They told me they wanted me return to the *Free Press* as its president and publisher. I told them I couldn't give them an answer until I discussed it with Phyllis, who remained under the impression that I had put the world of work behind me and that I intended to deliver on my promise of a carefree, travel-filled life in retirement.

The discussion with Phyllis was brief. She asked me how I was going to be able to say no to people who had said yes to me so many times for so many years. I said yes and came back to the paper and stayed until I turned sixty-five, retiring again in 1995.

When my return was announced, the only thing I could think of was how sorry I was that my mother was not alive to remind me of my beginnings and to warn me darkly that failure was still just a phone call away.

Phyllis stood in for her. When we agreed that I would accept the job, she kissed me and then said: "Not bad for a jumped-up copyboy. But don't let it go to your head because you know you can go down just as fast as you came up."

My mother, I am sure, would have smiled quietly at another circumstance of the promotion. For nearly two years during my time as city editor of the *Free Press*, 1965 until 1971, Jim Batten was one of my assistants, and he and his wife, Jean, became my good friends. I helped hire Jennie Buckner at the *Free Press* in 1969 following her graduation from Ohio State University, and she and her husband, Steve Landers, also a former member of the *Free Press* staff, remained my close friends. Because of all that, my mother would have seen their decision to make me the *Free Press* publisher simply as a logical extension of the "Favor in Hell" effect. In truth, I know how proud my mother would have been on that occasion because she was proud of all the good things that happened to her children and made sure we knew it. But she felt it was her duty to remind us to keep our feet on the ground, our heads out of the clouds, and to remind us to never, ever, forget where we came from.

My father, for his part, was less demonstrative in his reactions to the successes of his children. There was no question of his pride in our accomplishments, although we had to be able to read his subtle body language in order to get some idea of what might be going through his mind. When I was named city editor of the *Free Press,* I stopped by my parents' house to tell them about the promotion. My mother kissed me and gave me a hug and told me how proud she was. My father listened quietly while I explained what the job involved, the number of reporters I would be supervising, how only a half-dozen or so people in the United States were doing the same job on papers as large as the *Free Press*. When I finished, he smiled slightly and nodded. I knew he was pleased. We have to take approval as it is offered, regardless of how cryptic the communication might be.

As I continued to move up the ranks at the *Free Press*, my mother often babysat for us on nights when Phyllis and I had to attend a dinner or some other social function. Ma would show up at the house, see me in my tuxedo, and say, "Well, take a look at you. Off to rub elbows with our betters, are we?"

We're just going to a dinner, I would tell her, and they are not my "betters."

"Tell that to Henry Ford tonight when you see him," she'd reply.

I owned a tuxedo long before I had the nerve to tell her. I knew that if she found out I was no longer renting one from Mark Valente's Men's Formal Wear, she'd start believing that too much of the good life was beginning to turn my head. I could hear her reaction: "Your own tuxedo, indeed. Aren't we getting ritzy?"

When I told her once that I enjoyed a good, honest relationship with the people she called "quality," she asked me how many of them would be having a good, honest relationship with me if I was not a top editor at the *Detroit Free Press*. She told me some people would be nice to me as long as it suited their purpose, as long as I could do something for them. She told me not to mistake their demeanor for true friendship or an indication of their willingness to admit me to full membership in their circle. You're either born to it or you're not, she would tell me. You just don't fill out an application and join.

I saw all this not as the worst kind of cynicism but as an honest effort on her part to protect me from succumbing to all the flattering words and dazzling invitations and then somehow coming away from it all hurt and disappointed.

The truth was that I was acutely conscious of the social subtleties that governed rank and status in Detroit, and I always knew, in that grand scheme, where I belonged and where I felt comfortable. Long before she warned me about it, I understood that greatness by association was a false promise. But, unwilling to take my assurances at face value, she kept reminding me of my origins.

In 1988 the United Irish Societies named me Grand Marshal of Detroit's St. Patrick's Day Parade. When I told her, all she said was: "Boy, they must have been down to the scrapings this year." But she came to the parade.

In 1987 the Irish Pallottine Fathers, an order of missionary priests, informed me that they were honoring me as Irishman of the Year. They invited me to bring my mother to the dinner at which the award would be presented. When I called to tell her about the award and invite her to the dinner, she asked, "Aren't they the ones from Wyandotte?"

I told her that, as a matter of fact, their American operation was located in Wyandotte, a Detroit suburb, but their headquarters was in Dublin. The line was quiet for several seconds, and then she said, "Call me when they make you Irishman of the Year in Dublin."

If she detected even the beginnings of ego inflation, she considered it her role to deflate it. When the last of our children moved out of our house on Bedford in Grosse Pointe Park, I converted for my use as an office what had been sleeping quarters for our three sons on the third floor. I moved in a desk, my computer, and some file cabinets, and on the walls I hung a selection of plaques, proclamations, and medals that I had received over the years.

In truth, many of the awards were as much for longevity as they were for any notable accomplishments. I was given one honor, in fact, because the person who was originally supposed to receive it was unable to be at the awards luncheon and I happened to be available. The organization presenting it explained that it had planned to give me the award one of these years anyway and the last-minute thing was simply a matter of advancing the agenda.

But I thought the display looked very nice, not to mention what a comforting boost it was to my ego.

One day when my mother was over, I showed her my new office. She seemed more interested in what I had hung on the walls than in anything else. She moved from plaque to plaque, studying them, reading the citations, saying nothing. When she was finished, she told me she found it all very impressive.

"Now," she said, "on those days when it seems like the whole world's against you and you're moping around feeling sorry for yourself and surrounded by people who don't appreciate how wonderful you are, you can just come up here and look at your plaques."

She had a way of getting to the heart of things, a knack that sometimes gave me heart failure in social situations.

My wife and I gave a brunch on Sunday, January 27, 1974, for some friends. During the previous week I had met with Stephen Aris, a reporter from the *Times* of London who was in Detroit to do a story about the city for his newspaper. I had told him about the brunch and invited him and his photographer to attend if they were going to be in town.

They both showed up. The photographer was Anthony Armstrong-Jones, Lord Snowdon, husband of Princess Margaret and brother-in-law of Queen Elizabeth II.

If any brunch can be considered a success merely on the strength of a single person on the guest list, this one was off the charts. The brunch was from 11 a.m. until 2 p.m., but two o'clock came and went and nobody left, probably because Lord Snowdon showed no inclination to leave. We ran out of the inexpensive champagne we were drinking and had to send off to Alger Party Store for several more bottles.

I watched the clock nervously because my mother was coming over for dinner. It was her sixty-fifth birthday, and we had planned a small family dinner for her. I knew my mother and any member of the British royal family could prove to be a volatile combination, and I dearly wished his lordship to be gone before she arrived. My mother had been sitting for the children of a family whose parents were away for the weekend. She was coming to our house directly from her sitting job.

At about 4:30 she was dropped off in front of the house and came inside. Lord Snowdon was still there. As I was taking her across the room to introduce her to Aris and Lord Snowdon, I whispered, "For God's sake, behave yourself."

She whispered back just as forcefully: "Oh, shut up."

But she was a model of propriety. Her brogue was slightly more pronounced, but she was as sweet as she could be. The English guests were properly charmed. Then she picked up a bottle of André champagne from the table, held the bottle up, pretended to study the label, and said to Lord Snowdon, "I'll bet you don't drink a lot of this stuff at the palace."

"I can't say that we do, Mrs. Shine," he replied, smiling.

At that moment I thought to myself, "Oh, God. It's starting."

She put the bottle down and told Lord Snowdon that she had admired him for a long time, which was true. He thanked her.

"You know," she said, "I really think you're best of that whole lot."

"And what 'lot' would that be, Mrs. Shine?" his lordship inquired. He seemed to be enjoying where this all seemed to be going. I, on the other hand, was not.

"The royal family," she answered.

The room fell silent. Then Lord Snowdon spoke up: "Well, Mrs. Shine, you know that I'm related to 'that lot' only through marriage."

"And it certainly shows," she said.

I managed to move her away from Lord Snowdon, and she started talking to our friend Bill Somerset, who was with the British consulate in Detroit, which I saw as equally dangerous. I wanted her talking with people from the Detroit area, not people from England.

Somerset, a pleasant young man, was a career diplomat and eminently likable. I must have talked to him at some earlier time about my mother and her views on royalty. She was by no means an Anglophobe. She had four brothers and four sisters who, with their families, were British subjects and enjoyed a good life in England. But she saw the whole British royal family thing as a drain on the Exchequer by people who were entitled to live in grand style on government allowances simply because they happened to be born to the right parents. The common people put up with it all, she believed, because they were treated regularly to expensive displays of what she called "ceremonial silliness."

I think I may have told Somerset too much.

He said to my mother: "Am I to understand, Mrs. Shine, that you have no love for the queen?"

"That's not so," she said. "Love might be the wrong word, but I certainly admire her for the job she does. She carries an enormous burden, and I'm sure it's all very difficult. I respect her for the way she handles her responsibilities."

Somerset, pleased by her response, smiled and nodded.

That went well enough, I thought. This whole thing might not be as painful as I imagined.

Then, unwilling as always to leave well enough alone, Ma added: "But I'd never bend my knee to her. No curtsying, no bowing. None of that."

"You wouldn't?" Somerset said, not smiling anymore.

"No. But I'd be pleased to shake her hand, woman to woman, and tell her I respect and admire her, but I hear you can't touch any of the royals without permission."

Would you also tell her that you prayed for rain on the day she was married? I wanted to ask but did not. Things were getting bad enough without any help from me.

Somerset came right back. "Well, then, would you bend your knee to the pope?" he asked.

"I would not," she said emphatically. "I would shake his hand as well, tell him how much I respected him for the difficult job he has. But I wouldn't kiss his ring or bow to him.

"I spent the early part of my life curtsying and bowing, 'Yes, milady, no milady, right away, milady,' backing out of rooms with my head down," she said. She told him how she worried constantly about pleasing her "mistress" and how she feared her disapproval for even the smallest lapses.

By this time everyone in the room was listening to the conversation. She continued, telling Somerset about how the people in Carrick stepped off the footpath, tipping their caps and tugging at their forelocks whenever one of the gentry passed. If they, in turn, acknowledged the townspeople at all, it was often with a slight nod in their direction. "Getting away from that was one of the reasons

I came to this country. It's not what we do here," she said.

It was, we all agreed, a splendid statement.

Somerset was quiet again.

Then my mother said to him, "I'll tell you what I *will* do. I'll offer a toast to the queen."

She raised her glass of André and said brightly, "To the queen!"

Every glass in the room was raised smartly, and the guests responded in unison: "To the queen!"

People were taking their first sips of champagne when my mother offered this additional thought: "Up her kilt!"

People who felt it was impolite, if not impolitic, to laugh in the presence of the brother-in-law of the world's most prominent reigning sovereign repaired to the kitchen to laugh. Others laughed in place, taking a cue from Lord Snowdon, who was also laughing. I can no longer remember Bill Somerset's reaction. I can only assume he was not happy.

The party broke up about an hour later. Aris and Lord Snowdon were among the last to leave.

At supper that night my mother said she could not believe she had said what she did. "I honestly didn't mean to," she told us. "But I couldn't help myself. It just slipped out." Because she was our mother, we gave her the benefit of the doubt but for that reason alone.

The next day I was in a meeting at the *Free Press,* and my secretary opened the door and told me Lord Snowdon was on the phone. Several people at the meeting were properly impressed, although one editor asked me later, "Who was it, really?"

Snowdon told me he was leaving shortly for the airport and wanted to thank me for inviting him to the brunch. He said he had a splendid time.

I felt I should at least mention my mother's behavior.

"If she insulted you or hurt your feelings in any way—" He stopped me in mid-apology.

"Your mother is the most delightful person I have met in this country," he said. "She is a wonderful woman, and I have asked her to have lunch with me when she comes to London next summer to visit her sisters. I gave her my phone number."

I was stunned. I wanted to shout into the phone, "You gave her your phone number? Are you totally mad?"

But all I could manage was, "You did?"

"Yes," he said, laughing. "She asked me how she was supposed to handle it if Margaret answered. I told her she'd just have to do the best she could, and she said she thought she could probably manage it."

On the way home that night I stopped at my mother's house. I asked her if Lord Snowdon had given her his phone number at Kensington Palace. She told me he had and then went and got a folded piece of paper from her purse and showed it to me. He had written "Tony Jones" on the slip along with the number.

"Are you going to call him?" I asked.

"Of course not," she said. "All that stuff yesterday is fine in this country, but it's another story over there. They're pretty serious about all this royalty stuff."

I have thought many times since then that she would never again have had this kind of opportunity to mingle with the "quality" people. Not the mock gentry or the "squireens" of Leitrim but the real article. The House of Windsor. Inside Kensington Palace. I'm convinced it occurred to her as well when the invitation was being offered. It would have been a glorious chance to regale her sisters in Surrey—not to mention her family in America—about her day up in the palace with all the lords and ladies, the butlers and the footmen. We also considered the real possibility of an international incident with her smiling face splashed all over the front pages of the London tabloids: "HUGE RUCKUS AT KENSINGTON—AMERICAN GRANNY ROCKS THE ROYALS."

But she never seriously considered it, and it did not seem to be a difficult decision for her. She understood that Kensington Palace and the Cabbage Patch are more than just worlds apart. It all comes down to knowing who you are and where you belong.

Still, as in her tête-à-tête with Lord Snowdon, she was comfortable insinuating herself into places and situations where she was clearly out of her element and, most of the time, not among the invited.

She decided once when she was in London that she might enjoy seeing the Archbishop of Canterbury at work. Her view of world religions had broadened considerably since her first clumsy attempts to come to terms with the dietary laws of Judaism.

In 1981 she was visiting her sisters in Surrey and, with her youngest sister, Gertie, and Gertie's husband, Pat Gawley, had gone into London to shop. Her grandchildren were quite taken with rugby jerseys in those years, and she never returned from England without bringing enough jerseys to equip a small team.

"We had been down on Oxford Street," Gertie remembered, "and she had been in every shop where they sold rugby shirts to get some to bring home. By the time we were finished she had two big bags full."

She was always careful never to buy two jerseys with the same colors, something that required stopping at several shops. When the shopping was finished and they were walking to the station to catch the train back to Chertsey, they passed St. Paul's Cathedral. It was clear from the size of the crowd gathered at the front of the church that something big was happening that afternoon.

Police constables were trying to keep traffic moving around the long line of limousines depositing exquisitely attired people in front of the cathedral. My mother asked one of the onlookers, "What's going on here?" He told her it was the solemn consecration of the new Lord Bishop of London. She decided it was something she might like to see.

With Gertie and her husband trailing at a safe distance, my mother walked to the front door of the cathedral, approached the warder, and told him that she and her friends would like to go inside. She asked if there were any seats left. He told her there were seats left but she would need an invitation to sit in one of them. She explained that she was a visitor from the United States and did not have an invitation but suggested that it would be a genuine gesture of international goodwill if he let them in. They did not, she said, need a seat and were more than willing to stand. No one, he told her, sitting or standing, would be admitted without an invitation.

She had, by this time, decided that an event this important would most certainly involve the Archbishop of Canterbury, making her even more determined to get in, one way or another. Besides, the rebuff at the door, by a person she later described as "some stooge," was simply another example of a conspiracy by those she called "the quality" to deny the common people entry to, of all places, God's house. So she accepted the challenge as the self-appointed representative of the uninvited.

Not far from the front door she saw a man she decided was a functionary of some kind. She walked up to him and asked if there was any way that she and her friends could get inside for the ceremony. She was, she said, not getting any younger and was on what might be her last trip to England to see her family. What better memory would there be to take back to America to help comfort her in the twilight of her years? (She was seventy-two and actually made three or four more trips to England in the twilight of her years.)

The man politely explained that seating was limited and that not even all those usually eligible for such invitations had received them. He said he understood how much this meant to her and that he was terribly sorry but the rules had to be followed. He said he hoped she understood that there was really nothing he could do. She told us later that even while he was turning her down, she could see that his heart really wasn't in it. So she kept talking. She told him she was a religious woman who loved the pomp and ceremony of the church. She did not tell him that her religious activities were unrelated to the Church of England and that most ecclesiastical ritual in her life originated in Rome, not London.

She said the man reached into his inside coat pocket and looked

around nervously before handing her an invitation that would admit two to the ceremony. He told her that the people to whom it
had been sent were unable to attend and had returned it. He said
he was not supposed to give it to anyone else, but since it was clear
how badly she wanted to attend, he was willing to make an exception. She could go inside with one other person.

She told him God would surely bless him for this kindness and
waved at Gertie and Pat to follow her. At the door she handed the
invitation to the warder, and while he was still looking at it, she
poked her thumb over her shoulder toward her sister and her husband and said brightly, "They're with me," and breezed past him.

And so it came to pass that on September 21, 1981, Mae Shine
was present at the enthronement of the Right Reverend and Right
Honourable Father in God Graham Douglas Leonard, by Divine
Permission, 130th Lord Bishop of London.

As they walked in, the procession was beginning. The Great
West doors opened, and a fanfare was sounded. The magnificent
organ filled the church with music and the choir sang:

Praise to the Holiest in the height,
And in the depth be praise:
In all his words most wonderful,
Most sure in all his ways.

In solemn ranks the procession moved toward the altar beneath
the magnificent dome created in 1710 by architect Christopher
Wren: the crossbearers with their crucifixes; the taperers with their
candles; the choristers and vicars with their hymnals; the archdea-
cons of Hampstead, Middlesex, Northolt, and Hackney with their
missals; the bishops of Kensington, Stepney, Edmonton, and Willes-
den with their crooks and crosiers; and Mae Shine, sitting, watching, with her shopping bags.

It is not clear at what point in the ceremony she learned that
the Archbishop of Canterbury would not be participating in the

consecration of the new Lord Bishop. In his place he had sent the Archdeacon of Canterbury.

She was clearly disappointed. She told us later she would not have gone to all that trouble if she had known that the archbishop was going to send "one of his helpers" to stand in for him. She also said the new bishop should have considered the archbishop's absence an unpardonable slight.

"If it was me," she said, "I would have told them if the archbishop isn't coming, then you can keep the damn job."

But the Right Reverend and Right Honourable Father in God Graham Douglas Leonard took the job and kept it until 1991. He then left the Anglican Church, converted to Catholicism, and became a Catholic priest, a monsignor. My mother, who did not live to see any of this, would have, I am sure, traced it all back to the archbishop's snub. Push people far enough, she was fond of reminding us, and sooner or later they're going to push back. She would have enjoyed this particular push.

The Good Sport

Although she was hardly the 1940s equivalent of the soccer mom, Mae Shine was a loyal supporter of the school teams for which her sons played. She showed up every Sunday at Gallagher Field, at St. Jean and Kercheval, when I was playing football for St. Rose High School. She was not the noisiest mother in the stands, but I could always hear her. I was a determined but inept athlete with an absence of coordination, a condition quite possibly the result of my "arse backwards" world debut in 1930. Whenever I dropped a pass, which was most of the time, I could hear her shouting, "Just hold on to it!"

When I was in my forties and playing on a *Detroit Free Press* softball team, she came to some of our games at Northwestern Field. One afternoon, as I was trying to turn a double into a triple, I heard her again from the stands. "Slow down!" she was shouting. "You're going to have a heart attack!"

She was a Detroit Tigers fan, but I can never remember her taking the streetcar out to Briggs Stadium with us when our father took me and my brothers to Tigers games on Sundays, and she had only a passing interest in the Detroit Lions football team. But hockey and the Detroit Red Wings became her obsession.

In the early 1950s it was possible to buy a month's worth of tickets at a time, and once a month she would show up at old Olympia Stadium on Grand River and buy two balcony tickets for thirty days. Then she would repeat the process for the rest of the hockey season.

Sometimes one of my brothers or I would go with her, but most of the time she convinced a neighbor lady to join her. They would take a bus downtown and another out Grand River to the stadium, a trip of nearly two hours each way. The trip became easier when her brother Seamus moved in with us in 1958, and she quickly turned him into a Wings fan—more important, a Wings fan with a car.

She knew every player in the six-team league by sight, and she had scurrilous nicknames for most of the Wings' opponents. Carl Brewer of the Toronto Maple Leafs was "Ferret Face," Stan Mikita of the Chicago Black Hawks was "the Slinch," a word I think she created to denote a slimy reptile, and Eddie Shack, also of Toronto, was "Hose Nose," an unflattering reference to his most prominent facial feature.

Her seats were in the second row of the balcony, and she had absolutely no patience with people who stood up and blocked her view of the action. The first offense was always handled with a polite reminder that it was really not necessary for the people in front of her to stand because they were in the first row and nobody was in front of them to block their view. Then she would, with the same soft words, remind them that they had paid for the seats and they should seriously consider sitting in them for the rest of the game.

Second offense was an entirely different story. When, after having been duly warned, anybody in front of her stood up, she would take a handful of whatever article of clothing the miscreants were wearing—shirt, sweater, jacket—and pull them back into their seats. Hard. It usually did the trick.

Bill, a Detroit police officer at the time, was with her at a game one night when the young man in front of her, who had been given fair warning the first time he stood up, did it again. He jumped out of his seat at the precise moment the Red Wings scored a critical goal, which my mother missed seeing.

She took her purse, which was always heavy, swung it by the

straps in a wide arc and hit the man solidly in the middle of the back. He turned around quickly, his fists clenched, and leaned toward my mother. Bill, who was bigger and stronger than the man, grabbed him by the shoulders and pushed him sharply down into his seat. My mother turned to Bill and said sharply, "For God's sake, Bill, behave." Then she turned to the man she had just assaulted, apologized for Bill's behavior, and said, "You can see why I hate to take him anywhere."

The man, thoroughly confused by this time, nodded his acceptance of the apology and stayed in his seat for the rest of the game while his girlfriend rubbed the sore spot on his back. Instead of being troubled by it all, Bill saw the whole thing as simply a case of "Ma being Ma."

She was, in fact, a good sport in every way. As adults we teased her relentlessly. We suggested that we were often left to shift for ourselves while she was at Altar Society luncheons in St. Rose Hall or at meetings of the Ladies Sodality, the Catholic War Veterans Auxiliary, or the Daughters of Isabella, the women's branch of the Knights of Columbus. The more she protested, the more we teased.

We questioned her commitment as a mother, bringing up things like the "make some cheese sandwiches" note and the buckles on the bargain shoes she bought for Bill. He reminded her endlessly that all his subsequent foot problems could be traced to that pair of shoes.

I am convinced, for example, that she was sorry she ever told us about the times she left me, when I was an infant, in the care of the adult son of our landlady. We lived in an upstairs flat at 1190 Gray, on the East Side, and the young man, who lived downstairs with his mother, was mentally disabled. When my mother needed to go shopping, she would leave me for twenty or thirty minutes, she said, on the porch in my wicker buggy, telling the young man, "Now, John, don't let anybody come near the baby."

John stationed himself in a kitchen chair next to the buggy, holding a large butcher knife, menacing everybody who walked past the house, growling at them and waving the knife in their direction. She claimed that my erstwhile babysitter was a nice young man, and, though he might not have been "the full shilling," he was a person who wouldn't harm a fly.

Nor did we ever let her forget the night she left us home alone to deal with burglars while she was at the movies with Margaret Poisson. It was dish night at the East End Theatre. My father was still at work, and my mother put us to bed, deciding that we would certainly be safe for the hour we would be alone between the time she left and the time he got home. I was no older than eight.

During that hour a burglar forced the side door of the house and began to ransack it. Jim, who was six, and Bill, two, were asleep, but I heard the noise, walked to the top of the stairs, and called down, "Mom, Dad. Is that you?" The noise stopped, and I heard footsteps and the sound of a door closing. I went back to bed.

Jim's memory of the incident is that I sent him to call down to the burglars while I stayed safely in the background. His scenario could certainly be the more accurate one since it sounds like something I might have done.

The next morning we learned that the house had been robbed some time after my mother left for the East End and before my father got home. The net take was two dimes from a kitchen cupboard, a pair of hair clippers, and a case of empty beer bottles. Bill is still fond of reminding us that, even for that neighborhood, it was hardly the crime of the century.

My mother defended herself by arguing that we were much older than we claimed in our telling and retelling of the story. We told her that since we had moved from the house on Beniteau in 1938, the year I turned eight, we were giving her the benefit of the doubt on ages by assuming the break-in took place just before we moved. We also reminded her regularly that children's protective agencies remove kids from their homes and put them in foster care for offenses less serious than that one. She told us that if she had known what an aggravation we were going to be in her later years, she would have put us up for adoption and saved the state the trouble of putting us in foster care.

On her seventy-sixth birthday Bill and I showed up at her party without a gift, telling her that we had decided that a song written in her honor would be more precious than anything we could buy. We sang the song "Never Put Your Mother in a Home," while she listened politely, trying to act as if she were not enjoying it:

For your mother's still your mother,
Have her move in with your brother,
But never put your mother in a home.

When we finished, she called us cheapskates and then asked for a copy of the lyrics, which she had framed.

One of the items she placed in the green box was a 1969 note from Jim and a snapshot of a jetliner taking off. She had been to visit Jim and his family in Connecticut and was on her way home when Jim took the picture.

"That is your plane leaving LaGuardia," he wrote. "You can notice how it is laboring and listing somewhat to the left." She was, to be sure, no longer the wraithlike woman who resisted going to meet Aunt Mary before her marriage for fear of being judged "a doctor bill" waiting to happen. But if she was offended by this oblique reference to her weight, it was not serious enough to keep her from adding the note and the picture to her collection.

Bill has always had an active sense of humor, one that has not diminished with age. His presence as a police officer in downtown Detroit's First Precinct was a matter of constant concern for those who knew him. If he saw any of us on the street, he made a point of confronting us loudly, accusing us of any number of high crimes and misdemeanors in front of the crowd that inevitably gathered.

One afternoon a *Free Press* reporter, Carter Van Lopik, returned to the office talking about Bill in a most uncomplimentary way. Bill was actually a friend to most of the reporters at the paper, including Van Lopik, and a good police department source for many of them.

But on this day Van Lopik was returning from lunch when a police car wheeled to the curb and sounded its siren. Bill stepped out of the car, put his finger in Van Lopik's chest, and said, loudly: "I've warned you once about staying off Woodward Avenue, and this is the last time I'm going to tell you. Get the hell off Woodward, stay off Woodward, and if I see you on this street again, you're going to jail." Before the stunned reporter could respond, Bill got back in the car and drove off. By this time, Van Lopik said, the crowd attracted by the incident was watching him to see what he was going to do.

I asked Van Lopik what he did. "I got the hell off Woodward," he said.

Not even Ma got a pass from his antics. Toward the end of his life my father suffered from a number of physical ailments, the most serious of which was rheumatoid arthritis in his hips, and he was frequently hospitalized. My mother was visiting him in Harper Hospital one day when Bill and his partner showed up. They were working and in uniform and had stopped to see my father.

When the visit was over, they offered to drive Ma downtown where she could catch the bus home. Their police car was parked in front of the hospital. Flanked by the two police officers, my mother stepped off the elevator and into the crowded lobby. As they headed for the door, Bill grabbed her firmly by one arm and his partner took the other.

"Stealing from the sick," Bill said, loud enough for the people in the lobby to hear. "You should be ashamed of yourself." He hurried her out the door and into the backseat of the police car. She tried smiling as she was being bustled through the lobby, hoping the hospital visitors would realize it was all a joke. They did not. Bill said they just shook their heads sadly at the sight of this gray-haired woman being led off to jail but seemed reassured that she was going to have to answer for her crimes.

On the way downtown, Bill said, she called him several names, including bastard, something, Bill told her, that reflected as badly on her as it did on him. "It would," she said, "if I was really your mother."

On another occasion she was shopping at J. L. Hudson's downtown store when Bill, this time in plainclothes, walked up to her, flashed his badge at the saleswoman, and informed her she had just waited on Detroit's most prolific shoplifter. Before my mother could protest, Bill led her out of the store. Her anger at not being able to finish her shopping was softened only by Bill's offer to take her to lunch. After that day, she said, whenever she shopped at Hudson's downtown, she couldn't shake the feeling that every employee in the store was watching her.

We told these stories about her again and again, mostly in her presence, while she complained about exaggerations and fabrications, calling us ungrateful wretches who should be ashamed to admit, in front of anybody, the shabby way we treated the woman who gave us life and sacrificed so much for us.

The three of us believe that she saw all the teasing for what it was: a good-natured reflection of just how much we loved her. Indeed, she loved being the center of attention, and when we were around, we made sure that's what she always was.

Rarely does a day go by that I do not think about our life with her. She was quick to hit, quick to hug. She laughed a lot and smiled more. She was quirky and often outrageous. If the rules didn't favor her or her family, she modified them. Her approach to just about everything in life was, to say the least, unconventional. But, through it all, she never forgot the importance of being a mother. It was a role she embraced.

I think often about her gifts to us, about her substantial legacy. She made sure we understood that she expected us to behave—as children and as adults—in a way that reflected the values in which we were reared. She pushed us on our schoolwork, drilled a strong sense of right and wrong into us, and made sure we understood the difference. She could abide a lot of things in her children but impoliteness was not one of them.

She warned us that treating another child cruelly, with words or deeds, would continue to manifest itself in our adult lives and make us singularly unpleasant human beings. To join a crowd in taunting a playmate, she said, was the mark of a coward. To stand in defense of a person being taunted was a sign of genuine courage. Being gentle showed strength, not weakness.

She drilled into us the difference between right and wrong and did not let up until she was sure we understood. It was, to be sure, often her personal version of right and wrong, but it was, all things considered, remarkably close to the accepted norm.

The amount of good we did in our life was not what was important, she said. What was important was making sure we did it all the time.

She infused us with her gift of spontaneous humor and told us often that being able to laugh at ourselves was infinitely more important than being ready to laugh at others.

She was the core of our existence, a spot she never relinquished. We will never forget her, which I am convinced was always part of her plan. We are richer for having had our lives touched and shaped by her.

I worry still that we did not thank her enough for it all.

Epilogue: A Final Journey Home

Shortly after Ma's death in 1987, we had a small service in Mt. Olivet Cemetery during which we buried some of her ashes next to my father's grave. We brought the rest of her ashes home in a box that the funeral home provided, planning to one day all go to Carrick-on-Shannon to carry out her final request.

I put the box against the back wall of the high shelf of Phyllis's closet in our bedroom. Although I talked occasionally with my brothers about making the trip to Ireland, none of us ever had a sense of urgency about it. We were busy with our lives. So Mae Shine's ashes stayed on the closet shelf behind a stack of shoe boxes. We would do what we promised but not right away.

One morning in the winter of 1989 Phyllis asked me at breakfast, "Did you move your mother's ashes?" I asked her what she meant by "moving" my mother's ashes.

"In the closet," she answered. "Did you move them to the front of the shelf?"

I told her, truthfully, that I had not touched the box with my mother's ashes since I had put it on the shelf after her funeral, more than a year earlier.

She didn't believe me.

Somebody, she said, had moved the ashes from the back of the shelf, past the shoe boxes, to the front of the shelf.

When I was finally able to convince Phyllis that I had not touched the box since I put it in the closet, she said quietly, "We have to go to Ireland."

I called my brothers and told them what had happened. Neither accused me of moving the box. They agreed that Ma had been more patient than we had any right to expect and it was indeed time to take her back to Carrick-on-Shannon. We did so the following May.

We stayed at the Bush Hotel and brought her through the town one last time the next morning. Down the narrow streets of her childhood, past places remembered, places cherished. Past the shops where merchants were just opening their doors and rolling back shutters, arranging their wares on sidewalks freshly swept. Costello, Flynn, Dunne, Lowe, Doherty. Past Dr. Bradshaw's house, the place where she went to work at fourteen and left four years later, when she decided the world held more promise for her than this.

Even as children, we understood that some little bit of her never left this peaceful place she always called "lovely Leitrim." It was why she asked us to take her back.

We took her past the heavy doors of St. Mary's Church, where she had been washed in the waters of baptism more than eighty years earlier. She had been confirmed and made her first communion there, and it was the church where she had stopped on her way to the station that autumn morning in 1927, the day she was taking her first uncertain steps to a new life in America as a frightened eighteen-year-old.

We walked to the quay, in the shadow of the old stone bridge and next to the building where her father had supervised the unloading of barrels of Guinness barged up from Dublin, and prayed for her.

Then we sprinkled her ashes at the river's edge, no stone or monument to mark the place, just the timeless river being drawn down to the sea.

I have since read and re-read the words of Carrick's Michael J. MacManus. His poem, "Carrick," seemed appropriate for her final journey to this peaceful place.

O tired heart, take this one golden grain
Of comfort through the city's moil and roar.
Some quiet dusk you shall be home again
Where Shannon sings beside her reedy shore.
Beside the cool, green waters there will be
A garden waiting where the journey ends,
Birdsong, a flowering hawthorn tree,
And laughter and the quiet talk of friends.
What though tonight we walk through storm and rain,
Take comfort heart, nor heed the traffic's roar,
Some quiet twilight we shall hear again
Old Shannon sing beside her reedy shore.